The 77 Deadly Sins of Project Management

The 77 Deadly Sins of Project Management

𝖎𝖎𝖎 **MANAGEMENT**CONCEPTS

ⅿ
MANAGEMENTCONCEPTS
8230 Leesburg Pike, Suite 800
Vienna, VA 22182
(703) 790-9595
Fax: (703) 790-1371
www.managementconcepts.com

Printed in the United States of America

Library of Congress Cataloging-in-Publication Data

The 77 deadly sins of project management.
     p. cm.
  ISBN 978-1-56726-246-9
1. Project management. I. Title: Seventy-seven deadly sins of project management.
HD69.P75A27 2009
658.4'04—dc22

2009020009

10   9   8   7   6   5   4   3   2   1

Contents

Preface

Project management is a tough business. Not only do we have to contend with schedules, budgets, and a host of stakeholder demands, but we must also deal with sometimes vexing human behaviors—whining, indecision, opposition, inflexibility, complacency, and tunnel vision, to name a few. And there are more than a few. We've identified 77 "deadly sins" of project management that have serious, if sometimes amusing, ramifications for project work and the project work environment.

Our contributors are all seasoned project managers and team members, in addition to being experts in aspects of project management that include decision-making, leadership, risk management, earned value, requirements, and the work breakdown structure. They have focused on each of the 77 deadly sins and probed its manifestations and consequences for projects. By sharing their personal experiences, as well as some historical events, the contributors show us the effects and costs—both financial and human—of failing to get a handle on these sins and rein them in. They warn us of the danger signs, so we can spot a sin before it takes too great a toll on the project and the team. The solutions and tips the contributors offer at the end of each chapter will help us make sure that this particular sin doesn't derail or destroy our projects.

Of course, deadly sins do not usually operate in isolation; many are interrelated and tend to feed off one another. When the particular sin we are discussing involves another sin in some way, we highlight that other sin in bold—so you know what to tackle next!

The assessment tools that follow the chapters will help you zero in on the particular sins that are plaguing your current project and pinpoint the situations that are posing the greatest challenges. Use these tools to help figure out what to focus on and address first.

We have little doubt that you will recognize many of the 77 deadly sins on your own project. We hope that some insight, advice, and fair warning will help you keep them at bay and thus keep your project on track and your team progressing toward a successful outcome.

1

Acquiescence

Acquiescence is the act or condition of giving tacit assent; agreement or consent by silence or without objection; compliance. In project management, acquiescence can create a false sense of consensus.

The Sin

The best way to define acquiescence in the context of project management is to consider the Abilene paradox. The Abilene paradox is a management concept observed and articulated by Jerry Harvey, professor emeritus at George Washington University. It refers to the behavior of a group of people when they make a collective decision that is counter to the wishes of anyone in the group. Simply put, it's the tendency of groups to make decisions that no one individually really likes or supports. People in the group go along without questioning the decision because of fear, a need to conform, or perhaps an attempt to avoid **conflict** with the group or their superiors. The acquiescence, or tacit agreement, of each individual on a project team results in a decision that appears to be a consensus decision but in reality is not supported by the team.

Part of our social behavior, acquiescence is evident in social interactions everywhere. In organizations, acquiescence is usually an outgrowth of organizational culture. An organization that is very consensus-oriented, and that actively or passively discourages individual drive, is one that foundationally supports and could nurture harmful acquiescence. Interestingly, acquiescence can be manifested on projects positively or negatively.

Positive acquiescence is manifested when a project team is moving toward a decision, team members agree with the decision, and they give their tacit agreement through **silence** to expedite the decision. In such a situation, acquiescence is helpful because team members are supporting the operation of the project team through their behavior.

Negative acquiescence is manifested when a project team is moving toward a decision, team members do not agree with the decision, and they enable future conflict or disruption by giving their tacit agreement through silence. In such a situation, acquiescence is not helpful because team members are hindering the operation of the project team through their behavior.

A Case of Acquiescence

On agile teams, the person who represents the business organization is designated the "product owner." The product owner is responsible for maximizing the financial return of the product by defining business value, facilitating the creation of product features, prioritizing those features, and deciding the order and combinations in which the product features are released. The product owner's role is crucial; he or she must not only be knowledgeable about the business, but must also be empowered by the business organization to make decisions on its behalf. Because agile teams operate in short, time-boxed iterations or sprints, time is of the essence every day. Therefore, the speed of an agile team (and its success or **failure**) hinges on good decisions made quickly by the product owner.

One of the organizations with which I worked enthusiastically embarked on an agile initiative; unfortunately, they just could not seem to empower their product owners. Besides having a deep interest and commitment to its teams and associates, this organization had an overly consensus-driven culture. Any decision had to have the agreement of all parties involved, including almost the entire management chain of command. This meant that when a product feature was being considered, the product owner had to take the discussion back to management and get its approval before moving forward. The resulting lag in decision-making seriously hampered the team's ability to deliver customer value.

In this case, acquiescence on the part of multiple team members resulted in compliance with organizational culture to the detriment of the team. The project manager and other team members, although openly unhappy with the situation in team meetings, failed to raise the non-empowerment of the product owner as an issue with senior managers and other stakeholders in project retrospectives and reviews. The product owner and senior managers also gave their tacit agreement to the norms of the organizational culture, even though they knew those norms were in conflict with the rapid decision-making required for an agile approach to succeed.

The short-term cost of the problem was that project deliverables took much longer than necessary because of the delay in decision-making. The long-term cost of the problem was that the teams were not able to achieve the rapid, incremental delivery that agile methods are designed to facilitate, and therefore the investment in agile methods was not as profitable as it could have been.

Danger Signs

Acquiescence is a very difficult problem to identify, surface, and resolve. It sometimes requires active disagreement and even conflict on the team, which may not be comfortable for some members. To address negative acquiescence effectively, a project manager needs to understand each team member's personality and style. For example, if a team member who is usually loquacious quietly goes along with a decision, it might be worth taking that person aside and discussing the decision privately. Danger signs of acquiescence include significant decisions being agreed on by all members of the team too quickly and an increase in private conversations taking place outside regular team interactions.

Solutions

The problems caused by acquiescence can be hard to detect. Awareness is a key first step toward overcoming negative acquiescence. It's important to recognize that organizational culture and norms may be encouraging or rewarding this behavior.

The solution to resolving negative acquiescence lies in getting better at managing agreement. Primarily, project managers need to understand that this is more a problem of managing agreement rather than of managing conflict.

Tips for Addressing Acquiescence

▶ *Ensure that all affected team members actively contribute* to the discussion around team decisions.

▶ *Facilitate an organized discussion,* with each person getting an explicit turn to speak his or her mind, voicing at least one concern even with a decision they support.

▶ *Capture and circulate the team's agreement in writing* to avoid any misunderstandings.

▶ *Create an environment where team members are not afraid to speak their minds.*

2

Assuming

Assuming is taking for granted without proof, supposing, or postulating. We all need to make assumptions in order to simplify life and make decision-making more manageable. However, we must recognize that assuming is dangerous: We could assume something that turns out to be wrong. In project management, that wrong assumption could cause significant problems for our project.

The Sin

An assumption is a guess about the future (see **guessing**). No one knows the future with any useful degree of certainty, so we all make assumptions of various kinds to be able to make decisions about how to proceed. In daily life we make numerous hidden assumptions without realizing that we're doing it, and most of the time that is a perfectly safe and sensible thing to do. Sometimes we also make explicit assumptions, usually about the big issues where it matters if we get things right or wrong.

Projects take place in the future, and when we plan them we have to think about how the future might turn out. Just as in many areas of "normal life," there are lots of things we don't know about what the future might hold for our projects, so we have to make assumptions, or guesses. Projects involve several important types of assumptions, including:

▶ *Scoping assumptions.* For example, we may assume that our project includes the requirement to produce a full set of documentation, that it needs to be provided in English only, and that we can supply it in electronic format.

▶ *Planning assumptions.* For example, we expect all named members of the project team to be available when we require them, to stay on the project for the full duration, and to have the skill set they need to perform their assigned tasks.

▶ *Estimating assumptions.* For example, we assume that the cost of a novel task can be derived by multiplying the number of people on the task and a standard daily rate by the average number of days that this task has taken on previous similar projects.

Assuming takes place most often in the pre-project planning stages, when key parameters of the project are being determined, answering the questions of why, what, how, when, who, how much, and how long. It is common practice to record these assumptions in the project charter, business case, or statement of work, although in most cases this is not done well and the list of assumptions is usually incomplete.

Of course, in many cases it is quite safe to assume something about our project, particularly if the chance of our assumption turning out to be wrong is very small or if the consequence of a wrong assumption would be insignificant. But if we make an unsafe assumption about something important, our project could really be in trouble if it turns out that we guessed wrong.

A Case of Assuming

A well-known example where assuming caused a major problem is the case of the National Aeronautics and Space Administration (NASA) Mars Climate Orbiter mission in September 1999. NASA lost the $125 million orbiter because the contractor's engineering team used English units of measurement (feet and inches) while the NASA team used the more conventional metric system (meters and centimeters) for a key spacecraft operation. This resulted in a navigation error that pushed the spacecraft too close to Mars, and it consequently broke up upon entry into the Martian atmosphere. Each team assumed that the other team was using the same units, and no one checked.

Solutions

Fortunately there is a simple way to avoid committing the sin of assuming, by using the technique of assumptions analysis and linking it to the risk management process. Assumptions analysis involves three steps:

1. List assumptions

2. Test assumptions

3. Identify risks.

The first step is to list all the assumptions that have been made about the project. This requires the ability to think reflectively and creatively, as well as to be able to challenge accepted thinking. It is often useful to get the help of a skilled facilitator to assist in exposing assumptions by asking a series of targeted questions. It is important to find hidden assumptions as well as the more obvious ones (which should be listed in the project charter).

Next, the identified assumptions should be tested by asking two questions:

1. Could this assumption be wrong? (yes or no)

2. If it were wrong, would that have a significant effect on the project? (yes or no)

Some assumptions are perfectly safe and very unlikely to prove false (for example, we assume that our organization will not go bankrupt before the project completes), whereas others are less certain (for example, we assume that a key supplier will continue to provide the components we need). Other assumptions might turn out to be wrong but would have no real impact on the project. We are looking for cases where we have assumed something that could be wrong and where that would matter.

The final step in assumptions analysis is to take the cases where the answer to both questions was "yes" and turn those assumptions into risks. This can be done at two levels. The simplest way is to write a risk statement that negates the assumption. For example, we might have assumed that "All key project team members will stay on the project from beginning to end." If we determined that this assumption could be wrong and that losing a key team member would cause problems, we would write a simple risk statement saying "A key project team member might leave the project."

Alternatively we might decide to produce more detailed risk statements exploring possible reasons why this assumption could be wrong, for example, "A key project team member might decide to leave the company" or "A key project team member might develop a long-term illness." More detail is appropriate if the lower level risks have different probabilities or impacts, or if they require different response strategies. Otherwise, similar risks can be combined.

Tips for Avoiding Assuming

▶ *Perform a simple assumptions analysis* to expose any risky assumptions.

▶ *Use the standard risk management process* to deal with those assumptions.

3

Avoidance

Avoidance is the act or practice of withdrawing from something or someone. In project management, avoidance implies a deliberate act of moving away from something or someone, usually because it is unpleasant or problematic.

The Sin

One of my professors used to put it this way: "Eat your crow when it's young and tender, rather than when it's old and tough." In my experience, avoidance now leads to "old and tough" later.

Trying to avoid (that is, "ignore") potential problems on a project or **hope** they'll go away is counterproductive. You can't avoid scraped knees as a kid, and you can't avoid problems in the course of a project. What you can—and should—do is anticipate, mitigate, and manage problems as part of a disciplined risk management process.

Avoidance is the opposite of disciplined risk management, and since risk management is an essential element of effective project management, avoidance undermines the entire process. Worse yet, it makes way for small problems to grow into large ones.

A Case of Avoidance

It's like working with horses. Yes, horses kick, but the way not to get hurt isn't to avoid horses entirely. That might be effective, but it's not very practical if you enjoy being around them. People who are afraid tend to keep a good distance between themselves and the back end of a horse—they avoid getting too close, which is probably the worst thing they can do. A kick from a horse hurts the most at the "end" of its kick, when its leg is farthest from its body and moving fast.

On the other hand, if you stay close to a horse when you're moving behind it—better yet, if your hands are on its backside— the horse will know that you're there. Your chances of surprising the horse and getting kicked are reduced significantly.

Even if you do get kicked, you're so close in that the horse can't get much of a kick up, and not with much velocity. You could catch the horse's "early kick" hoof in one hand if you had to, and even if you couldn't, a short, close-in kick doesn't hurt nearly as much.

Project stakeholders and their issues are like this too, so keeping your distance from them isn't the smart thing to do. On the contrary, avoiding them entirely or pretending they don't exist is the worst thing you can do. If you stay close—close to the stakeholders and close to the issues—you have a chance to anticipate, mitigate, and manage them.

Danger Signs

A tendency to avoid shows itself early, particularly when a project manager doesn't set or support an environment where opposing views and ideas are aired openly. Open agendas can be dealt with, and when a view is out of sync with the majority of the stakeholder community, the smart project manager will bring in the sponsor to help reach a resolution.

A project manager who creates an environment where stakeholders feel like they're on the outside, and therefore don't feel welcome to share what they're thinking, is asking for trouble. Early issues will turn up as problems later on. The later they're dealt with, the more difficult and expensive they are to resolve.

Avoidance? Danger. Best response? Engage.

When you find yourself surprised by the question "Didn't you know that person X was offline on this?" you know you're too late. You've either missed signals or, worse yet, avoided when you should have engaged.

Tips for Overcoming Avoidance

▶ *Pull in all the stakeholders.* Don't allow anyone to avoid the issues. As soon as you notice someone missing meetings or failing to participate, go after that person and actively engage him. Use your sponsor for support if necessary.

▶ *Don't wait.* Act quickly to find out why someone has a question or issue and address it openly.

▶ *Embrace the opposition.* Don't avoid an idea or action just because it differs from your own. The most creative solutions often arise from entertaining opposing viewpoints.

4

Barriers

A **barrier** is anything that restrains or obstructs progress or access—a limit or boundary of any kind. In project management, barriers stand between the project manager and project success. Project managers today face more barriers to project success than ever before.

The Sin

One barrier to project success arises from the very definition of project success. In the 1960s, the early days of project management, success was measured entirely in technical terms: The deliverable product either worked or it didn't. During the 1970s that narrow definition expanded to include schedule, budget, and quality requirements, which became known collectively as the triple constraints of project management. During the 1980s the definition of project success expanded further to include customer satisfaction, and during the 1990s project success also came to mean maintaining the organization's work flow and corporate culture.

Another barrier to project success is the increasing complexity of projects. No longer can project managers achieve project success solely through their own efforts. Projects are more interconnected, more interdependent, and more interrelated than ever before. The businesses that conduct projects have become more complex as well, participating in more alliances with strategic suppliers, networks of customers, and partnerships with allies and even competitors. The usual project deliverable is no longer a stand-alone product used by a single customer; instead, projects are delivering systems for enterprise-wide use by groups of stakeholders with different needs.

The widening gap between employees and their executives in understanding project management also poses a barrier to project success. The international business guru Tom Peters has said that "all work is project work," reflecting how pervasive projects have become. As more and more employees understand project management and work in organizations that are increasingly project-based, they are frustrated by executives who don't understand project management adequately.

A Case of Barriers

A case in point is perhaps the most highly publicized software **failure** in history: the infamous Virtual Case File (VCF) project conducted by the Federal Bureau of Investigation (FBI). The VCF was supposed to automate the FBI's paper-based work environment, allow agents and intelligence analysts to share vital investigative information, and replace an obsolete automated system. Instead, the FBI claims that its contractor on the project delivered 700,000 lines of code so bug-ridden and functionally off-target that the bureau had to scrap the $170 million project.

Various government and independent reports, however, show that the FBI, lacking IT management and technical expertise, shares the **blame** for the project's failure. Specifically, a devastating 81-page audit released in 2005 by the Department of Justice inspector general, described fatal shortcomings at the FBI that can be categorized according to the three barriers to project success: an expanded definition of project success, increased project complexity, and the widening gap in understanding the discipline of project management.

The VCF project expanded the definition of project success, as well as complexity and scope, well beyond the traditional database-type boundaries with which the FBI had experience. The project expanded to include virtually all corners of the FBI and to involve enterprise-wide connectivity and functionality for 12,400 agents working out of 56 field offices and 400 satellite offices using 13,000 computers that were not capable of running modern software. The project was undertaken in an environment where the executives knew so little about project management that they assigned a person who had no IT project management experience as the VCF project manager.

Danger Signs

Recognition and screening require that at least some key individuals—if not the majority of employees—within the organization have sufficient project management experience and maturity to understand and be on the lookout for these barriers to project success. An early warning in the VCF project came from a member of the development team who questioned the FBI's expertise, the contractor's management practices, and the competence of both organizations. A security expert working for the contractor expressed his objections to his supervisor in fall 2002. He then posted his concerns to a web discussion board just before the contractor and the FBI agreed on a deeply flawed 800-page set of system requirements that doomed the project before a single line of code was written. His reward: a visit from two FBI agents concerned that he had disclosed national security secrets on the Internet.

Solutions

So, how can a project manager break through these barriers? How can a project manager achieve project success when that term has come to mean so many things that extend beyond traditional project boundaries? When the level of project complexity has ratcheted up so greatly? When more and more educated project managers are confronting executives who don't truly understand project management?

The simple answer is that project managers cannot keep doing what they have been doing and expect to succeed. The traditional control-based approach toward managing projects is becoming less effective. Under that approach, project managers sought to plan, monitor, and control the project. What could not be controlled could be influenced, and what could not be influenced could at least be surfaced and addressed.

Today, project managers must increasingly forge partnerships with executives who can help surmount barriers. For better or worse, project managers are highly dependent on executive leadership. Project success now depends on getting executives to help project managers overcome barriers. Instead of taking a passive approach by waiting for executives to determine project managers' needs, it is much more proactive and effective for project managers to tell executives what they need to be able to tackle project barriers.

Getting executives to proactively facilitate project success by helping project managers overcome barriers is an incremental and cumulative process: It does not happen all at once, nor does it occur in all elements of the organization or with all executives at the same time. Since this support requires certain behavioral changes, it is usually evolutionary. Executives and organizations have spent years becoming who and what they are. The good news is that the cumulative effects of modestly paced, genuine change are enduring. Those who understand the critical, dependent relationship that is necessary between project managers and executives have joined the evolution.

Tips for Executives to Help Project Managers Surmount Barriers

▶ *Organize and manage work as projects.* Project managers can feel like fish out of water when they work in an environment that does not organize and manage work as projects. Much of their effort may be spent trying to convince and educate stakeholders about the merits of project basics, such as requirements, baselines, schedules, and configuration controls.

▶ *Pick the right projects.* Picking the right projects can be as sophisticated as strategic portfolio management or as simple as selecting only the projects the project managers and teams have the capacity to conduct. Fewer projects are usually better—they allow project teams to spend more time per project, increasing the odds of project success.

▶ *Follow a written project plan and ensure that projects are based on documented requirements.* Project managers need adequate time during the initial project phase to build baseline documents, and they should be held accountable for continuous, controlled revisions to those documents throughout the project life cycle.

▶ *Require that cost estimates have a written, definitive basis.* Project managers must be able to manage the scope of their projects, and the key to scope management is a clear, mutual understanding of what is considered in-scope and what is considered out-of-scope. Providing a written estimate reduces the odds of a scope-related misunderstanding and also provides project managers a powerful method of supplementing their authority.

▶ *Ensure that project resources are commensurate with needs.* In return for managing their projects according to plan, project managers look to their executives to ensure that project resources are commensurate with needs. If resource shortages or changes occur, project managers should submit an impact assessment to executives—in an environment free of undue pressure to absorb the change or simply do more with less.

▶ *Engage middle management, and establish job definitions and performance standards.* By holding middle managers responsible for supporting project managers, and by ensuring that career progression and growth align with best practices, executives will create a long-lasting and sustainable project-based culture.

▶ *Behave like an executive and ask the right questions.* Executives can demonstrate their commitment to a project-based culture by behaving like executives and asking their project managers the right questions. By making a commitment to support project managers, executives will attract, retain, and build project management excellence.

5

Blaming

Blaming is holding responsible, finding fault
with, or censuring. In project management,
blaming is definitively and often acrimoniously
assigning blame for project failure.

The Sin

The reflexive, speed-of-light aspect of blaming others is part of our human nature: We are rational and we want answers. We assign blame, the issue is decided, and we can move on to the other 50 action items we need to accomplish . . . before noon. But blaming is never that simple.

Manifestations of blaming in project management include:

▶ *Project leaders not taking accountability for a business domain.* Who is a potential blame victim? Consultants! They can recommend best-practice options regarding what leadership should plan and measure, but senior management is responsible for defining the organization's strategic direction.

▶ *Project leaders not taking accountability for business benefits.* Who is a potential blame victim? Subject matter experts! They can provide elaboration of the business case for a chosen strategic plan, but senior management is responsible for defining the business drivers that will get the organization there.

▶ *Project leaders not taking accountability for business case metrics.* Who is a potential blame victim? The project management office! The PMO can provide dashboards on project execution success, but funding needs to be allocated to review whether the project is attaining the projected benefits promised in the business case.

A Case of Blaming

I was consulted on how to get some business analysts into shape. Reportedly their use-case template was a mess and their cycle-time was abysmal. In three days, I talked to 16 project stakeholders from all levels of the organization. I asked about the project mission, benefits, organizational challenges, and potential solutions. How much of the problem was discovered to be the use-case template? Almost none.

This industry gave great deference to the credentials of the product managers. The organization did not have a steering committee that arbitrated cost, time, and scope priorities. Two large, competing feature priorities were unacknowledged. Exacerbating this scope deadlock was the unbridled ego of the product managers. They had no intention of deferring to a business analyst and were free to articulate negative and dismissive attitudes about the business analysts.

Early in the project when there was one direction, the cycle-time for completing a use case was two days. With two conflicting priorities, it became difficult to define what the use-case process was. So the project office asked the outsource vendor to provide direction to the business analysts. This downstream development group threw the entire design and all the development deliverables into the requirements document. They burdened and slowed down the process to two weeks, and the business analysts were perceived to be at fault.

Danger Signs

Blaming instantly lowers project morale and increases employee turnover. Project challenges are significant enough without someone questioning your professional reputation and personal worth.

Blaming is an internal process. When it turns into external behavior, project success is at risk.

Solutions

Many project management sins are organizational or cultural issues. This one is personal. The solution is to control your emotions. If you don't control your emotions, when you feel under attack, you will reflexively become defensive and find someone to blame.

When we join a project, we typically are excited about being on the team and creating the product deliverables. When we see the challenges, we tend to worry. This is when the character of the project stakeholders is tested. Will those challenges be met with problem-solving behavior or with blaming?

All projects have challenges. So it is critical for the project manager to establish trust among all stakeholders when resources are brought onto the team. If trust and rapport aren't developed between team members, the moment the project encounters a problem, the blame game will begin.

Positive project behaviors that reduce blaming can be implemented by:

▶ Identifying all stakeholders

▶ Incorporating their requirements into planning sessions

▶ Implementing accountability through executive steering councils.

A basic marriage counseling principle is to change yourself before you ask your partner to change. Self-awareness and self-assessment can go a long way toward eliminating the sin of blaming from your project.

Tips for Eliminating Blaming

Recognize when you blame. Project teams don't need a weekend off-site retreat to do this. It is a quick process of self-evaluation. Especially when your emotions are engaged, check yourself for feelings of judgment and criticism. Stop and picture the situation from the other person's perspective or over a longer timeframe.

▶ *Recognize when you are at fault.* Great project managers are authentic and genuine. Have a sense of humor and humility if you have publicly expressed an erroneous or uninformed decision. Model humility and fess up to the thought process that got you here.

▶ *Recognize a team opportunity for improvement.* If you model open and honest communication, you will be in a strong position to ask your team to do the same. Payback in loyalty is immense.

6

Blinders

Blinders can be defined as something that obscures clear perception and discernment. In project management, blinders may be the result of internal personal issues or they may develop in response to the actions of other people.

The Sin

In the context of project management, blinders are any and all attempts to reject reality and to instead substitute some type of illusion. This illusion may yield a sense of increased safety, power, influence, control, or even **popularity**. However, by definition, it is always a false sense. Wearing blinders involves attempting to replace reality with some illusion that is somehow perceived to be less threatening or more comfortable.

Blinders are incredibly common in large organizations but tend to be less prevalent in smaller organizations. Small organizations simply cannot afford—literally—to tolerate an environment involving blinders because they usually have little or no reserve capacity (e.g., resources, cash, time, client base). Small companies typically live so close to the edge that they recognize, understand, interpret, accept, and accommodate reality—or they die quickly. Conversely, large organizations, possibly with substantial cash reserves, long-standing client relations, or established market dominance, can fall into a culture of rewarding blinders. In such situations, the culture becomes one where imaginary scenarios of good things that might be happening take precedence over dealing with the bad things that actually are happening.

Generally, any time there is a disconnect between what is truly happening and what someone thinks is happening, it is destructive to the team, the project, and the overall organization. Whether this happens at project conception, initiation, effort specification, solution design, development, verification, validation, or solution delivery, blinders tend to be fatal. This is a sin that, no matter when it occurs, nearly always results in some level of destruction.

A concerted focus on determining what is real, based on data, measurements, and other facts, is how engineers (e.g., systems engineers, software engineers, technology engineers, process engineers) strive to understand and respond to reality. Conversely, people who "believe" that they understand their environment, or who somehow "instinctively know" what is happening around them, are highly prone to not realizing when they are wearing blinders. Technology, ultimately, is an engineering discipline—not a religion.

The primary problem with blinders is that it is a technique by which you lie to yourself (see **prevarication**). The result is truly a disaster not only for you, but also for your team, project, and overall organization. As a result of blinders, your lies are completely convincing. Once you start to believe your own lies, so will many of the people you are working with.

When someone prefers to make their decisions and behaviors a function of illusions instead of focusing on reality, the results are not only unexpected but also typically far more adverse than any deliberately intended outcomes. Generally, a culture that rewards blinders is a culture that is ultimately conducive to repeated failures.

A Case of Blinders

On one project where I worked, the project manager was convinced that the best way to manage the project was by reacting to problems. The manager did not establish or document plans, track progress other than hours billed, or consult with any of the technical staff regarding potential scope changes. This manager's favorite solution to virtually any problem was to put an engineer on an airplane and fly him to the government facility, where he remained until the problem appeared to be fixed. Although our primary work was supposed to be occurring at our headquarters location, virtually no progress was being achieved on the baseline system because nearly the entire project team spent most of their time out in the field.

The manager on this project kept using the phrase "temporary crisis" during team meetings. However, it was clear to the rest of us that until the manager removed his blinders and saw what was truly happening, our "temporary crisis" was actually a permanent state of repeated failures.

Danger Signs

The most effective technique for recognizing blinders is carefully comparing actual results with planned results—or more precisely, the delta between the two. People who tend to respond to reality also tend to achieve intended and planned outcomes. However, for those primarily driven by blinders and other illusions, consequences rarely match intentions.

One of the danger signs of a tendency toward blinders is unsubstantiated optimism. As a test, you, as part of the management team, might present an interviewee with a set of scenarios that include difficult, nearly impossible, "no-**hope**" situations, and ask her what she thinks the expected outcomes would be. If she consistently responds with unlikely positive outcomes, then she might tend to wear blinders.

A second early detection technique is to carefully watch for evidence of someone repeatedly making the same mistake without adjusting her behavior. Such persistence in using a technique or strategy that is consistently failing can be a clear sign that someone has blinders on.

In any event, an organization is best served by realists, versus those who choose to ignore particular unpleasant details and who instead strive to make themselves "look" better, feel better, and live the illusion while simultaneously misleading everyone else.

Solutions

One technique for protecting the project from blinders is to lead by example. If you expect those around you to deal with reality (versus, for example, what you were expecting), then, as a project manager, you must take steps to be as fact-based and as evidence-driven as possible.

A second technique is to ensure that you recognize and reward people for the early detection of surprises, unanticipated developments, problems, and threats to the project. Similarly, find disincentives for attitudes and behaviors consistent with the use of blinders. For example, consider using several measures of project progress instead of just one. Likewise, use multiple criteria for determining successful milestone achievement versus, for example, a single pass/fail criterion.

However, the most critical technique for guarding against blinders is to detect them. Until you've taken this step, it will be very difficult to detect blinders in others. While most of us are motivated by hopes and dreams, when it comes to successful projects, we are typically best served by basing our decisions and behaviors on numbers, facts, and similar objective evidence.

Tips for Managing without Blinders

▶ *Don't work in* **isolation**—ask project team members and other stakeholders for their views, listen carefully, and ask for supporting back-up data.

▶ *Focus on evidence and facts.*

▶ *Strive to predict via documented plans how you expect the future to unfold;* then carefully monitor how well reality aligns with your plans.

▶ *Maintain a detailed revision log of changes* you make to the project plan and note whether revisions to the plan are becoming more or less frequent.

▶ *Implement comprehensive and effective risk management* and systematically review, analyze, and prioritize project risks while taking steps to mitigate the top-priority risks.

7

Bureaucracy

Bureaucracy is excessive multiplication of, and concentration of power in, administrative bureaus or administrators. In project management, bureaucracy consists of all the organizational processes that don't add value to the project (even though they may add value somewhere else). Bureaucracy is generally used to mean any organizational process we think is a pain in the neck. If we like the process or the process benefits us, we don't call it bureaucratic.

The Sin

The complexity and extent of organizational process tends to be proportional to the size of the organization. Big companies obviously need more process and more structure than small ones, making it more difficult to get things done.

In functional ("stovepipe") organizations, projects generally cut laterally across organizational areas. Bureaucracies tend to facilitate communication up and down their own chains of command rather than across those organizational areas, creating the potential for **conflict**, or at least additional project cost.

If an organization does relatively few projects, the environment has to be designed for operational work; project managers will encounter greater problems in getting things done because the system is not optimized for them. If the organization is mostly project-driven, the same bureaucracy may become destructive because it's no longer appropriate for most of the work.

Project teams are also subject to bureaucracy, and that's not such a good thing. A communications plan is a great tool to organize your project, but if you go too far, you'll spend all your time filling out forms and filing reports, and so will your team. When a project suffers from "hardening of the arteries," trouble can't be far behind.

A Case of [Positive] Bureaucracy

The Manhattan Project to develop an atomic bomb was intensely bureaucratic. Originally, a small group of brilliant scientists attempted to manage the project while at the same time directing the scientific effort. It was too much. Construction manager General Leslie Groves, fresh from building the Pentagon, was assigned to the job. He knew little if anything about atomic bombs, but that was not his job. Procedures and processes—bureaucracy—were the savior of the project. How else could three cities be built from the ground up (with every bit of infrastructure necessary, from schools to sewers), thousands of pages of military and contract regulations complied with, and the most complex research project in history kept driving forward?

Danger Signs

The costs of bureaucracy can be enormous. The wrong kind of bureaucracy can be even more expensive. Ironically, though, the absence of bureaucracy can result in a system completely out of control.

It is fashionable for technical people, especially, to disdain paper-pushing obstructionists, but by despising the people who hold your project in their hands, you merely solidify the problem. By refusing to acknowledge that their process often fulfills a legitimate organizational need, even if it doesn't benefit you and your project directly, you shut off any opportunity to find win-win solutions. It's okay to make a few jokes about corporate paper-pushers. If nothing else, some tension gets released. But distinguish between a little bit of venting and wholesale resentment—and help your team understand that compliance is simply part of the world of doing business.

Solutions

Bureaucracy is necessary and inevitable. Project managers have to accept the reality that not every system in the organization is—or should be—designed to benefit the project or the project manager. The killer is having a bad attitude or being inappropriately resistant to bureaucracy.

The vital project management skill set known as "office **politics**" has to come into play. The process of office politics involves dealing with bureaucratic structures and red tape unofficially as well as officially, using soft power and informal power to get things done.

Is that ethical and appropriate? Some people act out of selfish motives, and others use tactics that involve dishonesty or other forms of shady behavior. But you don't have to act that way to be politically effective. Listening, building relationships, considering the bigger picture, helping others and asking for help in return—these are the skills of a master politician (and project manager!).

Tips for Making the Most of Bureaucracy

▶ *Recognize that creating a viable organizational structure is a complex and sophisticated engineering project.* Learn to appreciate its value, so you can make sure that structure benefits your project, either directly or indirectly.

▶ *Use informal power to get the support your project needs*

8

Carelessness

Carelessness is not paying enough attention to the task at hand; not exact, accurate, or thorough. In project management, we must do everything we can to ensure that any after-the-fact review will not find a careless act we should have prevented.

The Sin

Carelessness covers a broad spectrum: from the carelessness of a child spilling a drink to the carelessness of a medical professional's malpractice. Although project managers do not usually work in life or death arenas, companies have high standards and expect professionals to execute projects as though they have lives in their hands. These companies expect exact, accurate, and thorough performance from their project managers.

Carelessness is common in project management, but the vast majority of the time it is trivial and goes undetected. Consider another common experience: driving a car. How common is carelessness in driving? How often do you forget to use your turn signal to change lanes, not come to a complete stop at a stop sign, or exceed the speed limit even for a moment? Do you feel that because no accident or ticket results, no carelessness was involved? How many other drivers have you seen exhibiting carelessness?

In project management, it is the patterns we set day after day that will eventually result in a project's success or **failure**: from the consistent carelessness of not capturing all the project requirements, to dismissively ignoring team member issues, to performing inadequate quality checks (see **shoddy quality**). Once a problem arises, it is easy to say that the problem couldn't have been prevented. But if you truly evaluate the practices leading up to the problem, you will often find a pattern that seemed harmless yet created unnecessary difficulty.

As project managers, we need to focus on eliminating carelessness—even if it is unlikely to have dire consequences—and thereby prevent project management malpractice.

A Case of Carelessness

An example of carelessness I have seen too many times in IT projects is poor testing of software. This is often traceable back to the original requirements. The project team develops and executes test scripts, but the scripts do not always take into account the original requirements. The software will pass the testing phase and move to production, but then bugs that were not screened out during the testing will pop up.

The customer loses the expected opportunity to use the software, and the project team must spend time and money to correct the problem.

The problems of carelessness are usually realized in the project's final stages. In this case, carelessness could have been addressed early in the planning phase of the project.

Tips for Combating Carelessness

▶ *Add and schedule tasks for developing appropriate testing* while the requirements are being identified.

▶ *Ask about and record how each requirement could be tested* during requirements gathering.

▶ *Exercise diligence* by not **assuming**—but checking and confirming.

9

Chaos

Chaos is usually defined as a confused, unorganized state or the inherent unpredictability of a complex natural system. In project management, chaos is the embodiment of the inherent unpredictability of a unique situation. It is the confused, unorganized state that results from the need to prioritize, plan, and execute a project that involves significant unknowns. Chaos can apply to either a specific project or an entire project portfolio.

The Sin

Chaos results from a host of project management problems. The list includes **failure** to involve users, lack of complete specifications, changing requirements, unrealistic expectations, incompetence, weak executive support, and insufficient resources, to name a few. Chaos is often self-inflicted but also can be caused by external factors.

Unfortunately, chaos is very common in project management, as affirmed by the enormous failure rate of projects in general. Since 1994, with the publication of the first *Chaos Report*, the Standish Group has been providing project management research, reports, and services about chaos. Apparently, there's no danger of running out of examples of chaos in projects!

Chaos in project management manifests itself in a variety of ways, from constant shifts in project or task priorities, to frequent replanning and restarting, to costly overruns in time and expense, to project cancellation. It results in wasted resources, frustrated staff, and dissatisfied users. In particular, personnel resources are wasted when their working environment is so chaotic that they are constantly forced to shift from one unfinished task to another task, which they in turn must leave prior to its completion to work on something even more critical. The mental setup and setdown time rarely is calculated, but most experts believe it is substantial. There is good multitasking, such as working on another task when the original task experiences an unavoidable interruption, but bad multitasking results in slower work and poorer quality (see **shoddy quality**).

Chaos in a project or process, if detected early, often can be corrected at little additional cost. If, on the other hand, a project that has been under development for a long time is abandoned, substantial resources have been wasted. Even when a project is completed, but completed late, an organization can lose competitive advantage, market share, or even a full line of business.

A Case of Chaos

My most serious exposure to project management chaos involved an organization's entire portfolio.

After a brief examination of current projects, I decided to review the organization's recent project management history. I could not find even one example of a successfully completed project—one that came in on time, with complete specifications intact, and at the budgeted cost. Many previously initiated projects had just faded away with resources no longer assigned to them, but not canceled, while others had morphed into new projects. This was project management in total chaos.

As this situation had been ongoing for some time, I could not come close to estimating the cost of lost resources in time and money. The consulting service was a quantifiable additional cost that the organization should not have required.

I did discover an interesting phenomenon. Interviews with several project managers revealed that they had much discretion in choosing the projects on which they worked. The staff had learned early on that they would never have to finish a project or be held accountable. If they lost interest in a project, they could just wait it out until something better came along. If progress stalled on a particular project, management always had something more urgent to be done—at least for a time.

Turnover was at a reasonable level and morale among the staff was fairly high. Management believed in a pleasant work environment and they had certainly accomplished that, but they were also concerned about not meeting their goals.

Danger Signs

The need to replan a project is a sign that either the original plan was inadequate or some unexpected force interceded. In any case, this is a circumstance that must be carefully studied for possible ramifications on other projects.

Management should review all staff reassignments. Someone leaving a project or looking for a new assignment prior to completion of his work can be an early warning sign that the project is in trouble or at least unpopular (see **popularity**) for some reason. The reasons for reassignment should be investigated and any underlying problems corrected.

Solutions

In project management, although we talk a lot about lessons learned, it is rare that lessons are actually passed on. We usually record the project problems and successes, but then we put them in the project folder never to be seen again. Project managers should review all previous project records and ensure that their own project lessons are recorded and accessible.

To avoid many of the problems that cause chaos, the project manager should use best practices that, to the extent possible, avoid these problems. Project management professionals know that certain rules and processes must be followed. They know that **deviations** from proven processes should occur only when absolutely necessary.

Several tools, such as earned value project management, can provide an objective measure of project progress. In addition, project managers must do everything they can to ensure that senior management has complete agreement and buy-in on basic and primary project management policies. If they fail in this responsibility, priorities will change unnecessarily, and so will the availability of resources. Chaos will reign—or at least rain on their parade.

Tips for Controlling Chaos

▶ *Use earned value project management software* or some automation tool that requires progress reporting.

▶ *Tightly control the number of concurrently authorized projects.*

▶ *Appoint a board member* (or committee) to be responsible for receiving project status reports at every meeting.

▶ *Discourage **dysfunctional** multitasking.*

10

Charity

Charity is usually defined as benevolent goodwill toward
or love of humanity, generosity and helpfulness toward
the needy or suffering, or aid given to those in need.
It can also mean lenient judgment of others. In project
management, charity can take the form of doing favors.

The Sin

We all have been in the situation where a customer or team
member asks to add a feature or upgrade the quality of a certain
item. We often agree to do these favors because we find ourselves
unable to say "no"—driven by our desire to please or a precon-
ceived notion that we do not have that option. Doing favors on
projects can carry a high price if the project is delayed or its costs
increase.

Charity manifests itself on projects in different ways. On the
positive side, it can give team members more life balance by allowing them to refuse overtime or reward the team for project
successes by distributing gift vouchers for a job well done. This

type of charity pays for itself in a more motivated team, resulting in higher productivity. On the negative side, charity can manifest itself in symptoms like scope **creep**, unrealistic expectations, and keeping unqualified or non-performing team members.

Charity on projects happens because many of us like to help other people. Doing so makes us feel good. Saying no or making tough decisions can make us uncomfortable. The problem with doing favors is that it can have a domino effect or even start the project on a downward spiral. One favor begets another and before you know it, you have lost control over the project scope, budget, or timeline.

A Case of Charity

I worked on a project to customize and implement an enterprise resource planning (ERP) system. By the time I got involved, the standard off-the-shelf product had been modified through 14,000 hours of customization work, the majority of which was spent meeting requests for "favors." The result of so much customization being done as favors was "spaghetti" code.

My concern about the performance of the software after go-live led me to ask a third party to conduct a project audit. This outside party advised me to stop the project and re-evaluate the work done, since there was a high likelihood that the software would fail after a few months of use. I took this advice to the project sponsor, who disregarded it for fear of losing face. I escalated the issue to my VP, who assured me that everything was fine (after providing charity—that is, allowing scope creep—during a game of golf with the project sponsor). The software went live as planned but became unusable after six months. The rework required and the end users' loss of productivity ran into the millions of dollars.

Danger Signs

Charity happens in every organization and on every level. The key is to distinguish good charity from bad and to make the latter visible before resources are committed. Sometimes that is all you can do, as in the ERP case. However, you may be able to slowly change the organization to one with an open communication culture where charity is fully understood and accepted when it makes sense within the project boundaries. In this way, charity will no longer be a "sin."

Solutions

The construction industry has made controlling charity an art. Anyone who has ever built a house or done some remodeling knows that contractors do not do charity. Any requested change is discussed, the work estimated, a cost assigned, and a new timeline approved.

Project managers in other industries would do well to take a lesson from the construction industry. Rather than simply saying no when someone requests charity, make the price tag visible so that the right decisions and tradeoffs, if required, can be made. Skillful project management is not about trying to please one person at a time; rather, it is about satisfying the majority of the project stakeholders involved. This requires balancing all expectations.

Tips for Conquering Charity

▶ *Manage the expectations of your stakeholders.* Communicate to your team, your client, the end-users, and other stakeholders the potential costs of changes and additions, and explain that charity will not be extended on your project.

▶ *Understand that change is a given on projects and people will always ask for favors.* The goal is not to stop changes, but to make the impact of requests visible so an informed decision can be made.

▶ *Do not strive to be liked by everyone. It is human nature for most of us to want to please.* Your job as a project manager is to manage the agreed-upon scope, budget, and timeline, and of course, your stakeholders' expectations. Project management is not a **popularity** contest.

▶ *Make tough decisions.* If you have team members who are not performing or are not the right people for the job, work with them and their managers to have them moved to another project (or fire them if they are contractors). It is not in the best interests of the project to keep them on the project team just because you like them or feel sorry for them.

11

Close-Mindedness

Close-mindedness is intolerance of the beliefs and opinions of others; being stubbornly unreceptive to new ideas. In the context of project management, close-mindedness is the hallmark of the command-and-control project manager, who makes decisions unilaterally or with only one or two others who have similar views and perspectives.

The Sin

Unfortunately, close-mindedness is all too common on projects. Our inclination, and much of our training, is to manage projects using traditional reductionist, control-based methods.

The paradigm we use to manage projects goes something like this: If we can decompose the work effort into manageable chunks of work applying reductionism (which postulates that complex systems can be completely understood in terms of their components), we can reduce complexity and risk, develop a plan, and then execute and rigorously control changes to the plan. Once the plan is developed, the project manager inevitably becomes close-minded, not wanting any changes to derail the schedule. Even changes that add business value to the solution are viewed as "scope **creep**" rather than as new, improved ideas. The result is that project team members are treated as worker-bees who are expected to mindlessly build solution components within the schedule and budget constraints.

A Case of Close-mindedness

On a recent project, the project manager set herself up as the only one who talked to the client, isolating the team from involvement (see **isolation**). The project manager made decisions unilaterally or with only one or two like-minded team members. In addition, she became very controlling when working with both the client and the team; as a result, the team became **dysfunctional** (e.g., arguing, finger-pointing, isolating key members) and the client became more and more dissatisfied.

When issues were brought to the project manager's attention, she was too close-minded to listen to concerns raised by the team members. Costs to the project included:

▶ Poor morale, forced overtime, rework

▶ Compromised quality of the deliverables due to last-minute delivery and refusal to involve all key players in quality reviews (see **shoddy quality**)

▶ Lowered perception of the organization's ability to manage projects well and ensure client satisfaction

▶ Confused and disappointed client.

Danger Signs

Typically, close-mindedness is most destructive early in a project, when brainstorming, innovation, and creativity are needed to determine the most effective and feasible solution to the business problem. When all key project team members are involved in analyzing the business problem and opportunity, identifying solution options, and molding the most feasible approach, the project is likely to be off to a positive start. However, with a close-minded project manager who is uncomfortable with ambiguity, early project decisions are made in isolation to expedite the kickoff of project work. Then, as project team members begin to offer suggestions, the close-minded project manager is likely to be frustrated at the perceived lack of cooperation.

The most effective way to screen for close-mindedness is to ensure that individuals who are placed in project manager positions understand how to form, build, sustain, and lead a high-performing team. As leaders of teams, project managers need to understand the stages of team development in order to develop and use an appropriate management style. Command-and-control is almost never appropriate. Rather, a facilitative, consultative approach to leading a team will enable the most creative solutions to emerge. Leadership skills such as negotiation, **conflict** management, problem-solving, cost-benefit analysis, group decision-making, facilitation, and collaboration are critical, as is business-outcome thinking. In addition, when red flags emerge, management needs to be open-minded in its efforts to discover what is really happening.

Solutions

Project leader development must be considered carefully. Project management training and certification are essential, but only lay the foundation for performing project management activities. New project managers should serve in a support role, working with accomplished project professionals. In addition, on-the-job support and mentoring are essential for all project leadership roles.

To create a world-class project manager development program, a career path is a vital tool. Training courses and professional development opportunities can build the competencies and proficiencies needed to fulfill responsibilities at each level.

Career Path Level	Proficiency	Responsibilities	Competencies
Strategic	Ability to perform strategic tasks with minimal direction	Lead large, highly complex projects	• Business and IT strategy • Program and portfolio management • Systems engineering, business process reengineering, Six Sigma • Enterprise architecture • Business case development • Leadership and management
Senior	Ability to perform complex tasks with minimal coaching	Lead moderately complex projects	• Business and IT domains • Advanced project management and business analysis • Systems engineering, business process reengineering, Six Sigma • Requirements engineering and management • Team leadership
Intermediate	Ability to perform simple-to-moderately complex tasks with minimal assistance	Lead small, independent projects	• Business or IT domain • Fundamentals of project management and business analysis • Quality management • Facilitation and meeting management • Basic requirements modeling
Associate	Ability to perform simple tasks with assistance	Support intermediate and senior project managers/business analysts	• Project management principles • Business process reengineering, Six Sigma • Business writing • Working in teams

Project managers and other project team leaders (business analysts, architects, lead developers, business visionaries) working together collaboratively to deliver the most valuable business solution are needed to manage today's complex projects. The close-mindedness of the traditional command-and-control version of project leadership can no longer be applied if we want to improve project performance and meet the challenges of the 21st century.

Tips for Addressing Close-mindedness

▶ *Have senior project managers serve as mentors* to junior and intermediate project managers.

▶ *Establish project management forums or communities of practice* where lessons learned and best practices can be shared and issues can be resolved in a collaborative environment.

▶ *Offer project management training* accompanied by leadership, management, and team-building training.

▶ *Conduct workshops using actual projects as case studies* on subjects such as strategic communication, managing cultural and political obstacles, managing change, and group decision-making.

12

Cluelessness

Cluelessness typically means a lack of understanding or knowledge—the state of being totally uninformed about something or not having any idea what is happening. In project management, cluelessness refers more to a lack of awareness than a lack of information, and it can have a significant effect on project success and team morale.

The Sin

In the early 19th century, Franz Liszt, the great Hungarian pianist and composer, was performing a concert when the Russian czar, Nicholas I, made a rather noisy, grand entrance. Even after he had been seated, Nicholas continued to talk loudly with members of his entourage, disturbing not only the musicians but also the audience. Liszt, realizing that Nicholas had no intention of being quiet, stopped performing and bowed his head. Nicholas, noticing the silence, sent one of his aides to find out why the concert had ended. "Music herself should be silent when Nicholas speaks," Liszt responded. Nicholas greeted Liszt's message with a nod and a brief smile and sent the aide back with a request that

Liszt continue the concert. Liszt obliged and finished performing for a captive audience, including the now-quiet, attentive czar.

Project managers who commit the sin of cluelessness are often like Nicholas—unaware of the consequences of their behavior. Cluelessness refers to a lack of awareness, not merely a lack of information, and it can affect project success and team morale. Nicholas didn't realize his antics would cause the concert to end. Liszt courageously and tactfully gave Nicholas a clue, and Nicholas listened, learned, and changed his behavior. Regrettably, some clueless project managers and team members don't learn and change as quickly as Nicholas did.

A Case of Cluelessness

One case of cluelessness involved a newly hired senior official; let's call her "Bea." Bea was full of energy and enthusiasm, but she was also notoriously clueless. The company she worked for, Mucho Grande, had a reputation for honesty and fair play that had been built over many years. Customers trusted the company, and Mucho Grande's employees were proud of the company's reputation.

One of Bea's first initiatives was to change resource management providers. Mucho Grande had outgrown the level of resource management services provided by Mid-Size Resources, so Bea asked Large-Size Resources to prepare a list of services it could provide. The CEO of Mid-Size got wind of Bea's request and inquired about it. Bea assured him that everything was fine and that Mid-Size would have a fair opportunity to compete for the work. Bea secretly asked Large-Size to assist in the preparation of a request for proposals (RFP) that Mucho Grande then issued only to Large-Size, giving the company a two-week deadline.

On the Friday afternoon before the Monday-morning deadline, Bea sent the RFP to Mid-Size. On Monday morning, Bea declared the hurriedly prepared proposal from Mid-Size inferior to the proposal provided by Large-Size and awarded the contract to Large-Size. When the CEO of Mid-Size complained about the way his company had been treated after 10 years of service, Bea honestly didn't have a clue why the CEO was angry. She had simply pursued a goal to upgrade resource management providers, so what was the problem? Bea had not given Mid-Size a fair chance to win the contract, but she had accomplished her objective and was then ready to move on to her next project. It wasn't personal—it was just business. What she didn't realize was that she had just damaged Mucho Grande's reputation for honesty and created an environment of distrust among Mucho Grande's customers, clients, and staff.

The consequences within Mucho Grande were devastating. Once word leaked about the way Bea had treated Mid-Size, Mucho Grande staff felt disgusted and began to question their continued association with the company. Two key staff members resigned and those who remained started looking over their shoulders, wondering if they would be the next victim of Bea's cluelessness. Senior leadership, finally tiring of Bea's actions, fired her—and she never understood why.

Bea had become successful because she met her deadlines, generated a healthy revenue stream from her contracts, and was more than a little intimidating. She was a bit rough around the edges, and some senior managers thought she was more trouble than she was worth. Nevertheless, as the old Woody Allen joke goes, management decided not to convince her she wasn't a chicken because they needed the eggs.

Unfortunately for Bea, nobody helped her understand her faults and their consequences early in her career, and as she was promoted over time, fewer and fewer people were in a position to advise her. Instead of confronting her, Bea's superiors ignored the problem and thereby enabled her bad habits.

Tips for Keeping Cluelessness at Bay

▶ *Explain to a clueless employee why a particular action was inappropriate* and had significant consequences. If clueless people can learn to think before they act, perhaps by finding someone to consult before they take actions that might have unintended consequences, they may be able to learn to act more appropriately.

▶ *Minimize the damage.* Sometimes you end up with clueless people on your team because of a corporate policy that assigns "deadheads" (not the Grateful ones) to a project just to keep them billable until they can be replaced by more qualified personnel. There may not be anything you can do to change the corporate policy, but you can try to minimize the damage caused by a clueless team member—perhaps by putting him or her in a corner and withholding important assignments and sharp objects!

▶ *Do not let cluelessness slide* and **hope** someone else will take responsibility for the consequences.

13
Complacency

Complacency is defined as a lack of awareness of actual deficiencies or dangers. In project management, complacency is the inability to recognize potential risks to project success.

The Sin

Like heart disease in human beings, complacency is a common "silent killer" of projects. Generally, there are no warning signs that it is about to occur—or is already occurring—on the project. Project managers can easily be lured into complacency without even realizing it. Thus, this sin often goes unrecognized until it's too late.

Complacency most often occurs when everything is going great on a project—ahead of schedule, under budget, and meeting the client's expectations. When things are going well, the project manager can be lured into feeling invincible. Pleased that the team is performing at a high level and feeling like nothing can go wrong on the project, the project manager can lose focus and concentration on the potential risks that may lie in wait. When a project leader puts down her guard and becomes complacent about how the project is progressing, unforeseen risks can rear their ugly heads and negatively affect the project.

Not only can complacency lead to thousands, possibly millions, of dollars being lost on a project, but it can also have long-term effects on the organization. For example, when a project is running smoothly and then all of a sudden takes a nose dive, the negative impact on the morale of the project team, as well as the organization, can be devastating. The results can include high turnover, lack of trust in the project's and the organization's leadership, increased administrative and project oversight requirements, closer scrutiny by executive leadership, and high stress levels for anyone willing to take on the role of project manager.

A Case of Complacency

One of the areas where complacency often occurs on a project is in the identification and management of stakeholders. Some years ago I was managing a large construction engagement that was progressing smoothly with very few problems and none to be seen on the horizon. It was at the point when we thought everything was going as well as it possibly could that an unforeseen risk jumped up and stopped the project dead in its tracks. Apparently, the project team had overlooked an environmental activist group in the stakeholder identification process and had therefore not considered this potential risk to the project. Suddenly, this group was able to halt all work on the project until its needs and concerns had been addressed.

Our complacency led to thousands of dollars in delays and legal fees on the project, causing the project to be delivered behind schedule and over budget. Complacency had led the project team to think that everything was golden and nothing could go wrong. The team lost focus and didn't see the risk coming until it was too late.

Danger Signs

Complacency is the silent killer of projects. Generally, the team's complacency is not recognized and an issue arises with no forewarning. Once a project manager realizes that the project is in trouble, it is often too late to take corrective action. If there is any warning sign for the project manager, it is when everything is going great on the project and it seems that nothing can go wrong. When this happens, the project manager should be on the highest alert for any risks that may have been overlooked or new risks that may occur.

Tips for Confronting Complacency

▶ *Be alert and stay focused* on every aspect of your project, particularly when things are going well.

▶ *Constantly re-evaluate the identified risks* to the project and investigate whether any new risks have arisen since the last review period.

▶ *Examine and report the project's status*, even when the project has no significant issues.

▶ *Consider having an independent party review or audit the project.* Sometimes we get so close to the project that we can't anticipate problems until it's too late.

14

Conflict

Conflict is a state of disharmony between incompatible or antithetical persons, ideas, or interests; a clash. In project management, conflict becomes a "sin" when it is ignored or allowed to simmer and fester into something destructive.

The Sin

Not only is conflict common, but it is to be expected on a project. Individuals from differing backgrounds and cultures, with their various belief and value systems, make the project environment rife with opportunity for conflict. Successful project completion requires that the project manager become adept at—and fully involved in—the art of interpersonal communication. When ignored and allowed to fester, conflict can lead to frustration and has the potential to create active subversion on the project team.

Conflict is to be expected throughout a project's lifecycle. In the early stages of a project, some level of conflict is actually necessary to help the team become cohesive and perform exceptionally. During these early stages, trust may be built through conflict. Conflict arising near the end of the project, during the implementation or testing stages, tends to be more destructive to the project and to the team. This late-stage conflict usually stems from incompatible or misunderstood requirements gathered at the beginning of the project.

A Case of Destructive Conflict

Early in my project management career, I was assigned to manage a project to test a new server platform. To conduct the testing, two labs in different locations were required to collaborate on approach, strategy, and planning. At the time, I was unaware of the long history of contempt between these two organizations. To make matters worse, the project was being performed in a time of company downsizing and each lab director was lobbying for recognition as the testing center-of-excellence for all products.

As a result of the rivalry between the lab directors, the project was ultimately eight months late to deliver. The increased time-to-market led to lower profits. In addition, team morale suffered. Because each director was acting in a dictatorial way, my project team became very apprehensive about interacting with either of them. The irony is that this interaction was critical for the project to succeed. In the end, a senior vice president had to remove one of the lab directors from his position.

Danger Signs

Project managers need to continually monitor for the warning signs of conflict. Most signs are nonverbal. In meetings or face-to-face communications with stakeholders, pay close attention to body language such as closed postures (e.g., crossed arms or legs), inability to make eye contact, or eye-rolling. These are sure danger signs of **misalignment**, **miscommunication**, misunderstanding, and conflict. Early in the lifecycle of a project, pay close attention to interpersonal communication and behaviors. Some people simply do not work well together and this should be considered in team composition. If possible, work with resource managers to get your project staffed with compatible people.

Solutions

A project manager should expect conflict on projects. In fact, during the more creative phases of a project (typically the early stages), conflict should be fostered to ensure that the best ideas are heard and that they are properly vetted across the team. A useful practice is to take a team personality assessment such as the Meyers-Briggs Type Indicator (MBTI®) or the Birkman personality assessment. These tools are useful for helping project managers understand the strengths and weaknesses of individual team member personalities so each may be used appropriately on the project. For example, leverage your sales-type person to sell the project; it would make no sense to use a planner type to do this.

Tips for Dealing with Conflict

▸ *Perform a comprehensive stakeholder analysis early in the project.* If I had done so in the case of the competing lab directors, I would have realized what was going on and possibly been able to divert some of the interactions that led to heated debate and destructive conflict.

▶ *Be cognizant of your communication style and content,* as communication both breeds and resolves conflict.

▶ *Address conflict immediately.* Left unaddressed, conflict does not go away; it only becomes more destructive.

▶ *Focus on the positive points in conflict.* Seek common ground among those in conflict; situations can usually be turned into positives if handled properly.

▶ *Be slow to anger.* Anger is a certain way of diverging from the intersection of common interests.

15

Confusion

Confusion is the act of disorder, upheaval, tumult, or chaos. In project management, confusion occurs when the members of the project team and the stakeholders are not in sync regarding project goals and the processes and methods planned to achieve those goals.

The Sin

Henry Miller, the American novelist, once said: "... confusion is a word we have invented for an order that is not understood." Confusion is the result of a lack of effective communication and, in project management, often a lack of experience working in a project environment.

Confusion is common to all projects to some degree because human nature ensures that there can never be perfect communication between the project manager and the members of the project team. Misuse of resources is the primary manifestation of confusion, in particular when team members spend time and effort on activities that are not productive. Confusion arises when not all team members have the same understanding of the project manager's priorities and path to achieve the project goals. The amount of confusion varies with the experience of the project manager and the team members. Robert McCloskey, the American author and illustrator of children's books, summed up the problem, perhaps a little too well, when he said: "I know that you believe you understand what you think I said, but I'm not sure you realize that what you heard is not what I meant."

Some degree of confusion is to be expected at the beginning of a project. An experienced project manager will work rapidly to eliminate confusion by communicating clearly with the team members in team meetings and individually.

Confusion is most costly as the end of the project nears, when the work to be performed and the priorities should be clear. Confusion at this stage will likely result in a **failure** to meet the important goals of the project, including cost, schedule, and performance.

A Case of Confusion

I recently worked on a project to help a company prepare a proposal to the U.S. Navy. This was not the first time I had worked with this company or the first time I had worked on a proposal for the same product. However, it was the first time I worked in this plant. Although the project manager and I clearly understood my role on the project, there was major confusion within the ranks of the individuals I needed for support as well as on my part about how I was going to get support. While cooperative, these individuals were not used to outsiders coming into their plant, and the project manager had not met with them to explain the situation. Therefore, they tended to wait until they were given a specific detailed assignment. Each assignment involved a long discussion of not only what was needed but also why it was needed. This confusion seriously hampered our ability to produce the project end item—the proposal—on time and threatened the quality of our work as well (see **shoddy quality**). The confusion was resolved by a series of individual meetings with each person from whom input was needed.

In addition to the confusion among the individuals who were supposed to work on the proposal, there was confusion regarding the physical resources I needed to have available, such as printers, Internet access, and copy machines. Although I had specified these in advance, none were available when I arrived at the plant. I assumed my hosts were confused regarding my requests when, in fact, they had decided to wait until I arrived to see what I really needed.

The costs of these problems were all measured in terms of time—the time available for actual preparation of the proposal. Reduced time potentially translates into lower quality.

Danger Signs

The potential for confusion exists in all projects. It is up to the project manager to quickly provide clear direction to all involved. Until this occurs, work will be inefficient at best (see **inefficiency**). At worst, work that is contrary to the interests of the project may be performed.

Danger signs of confusion are idleness (caused by lack of clarity about what is wanted) and lack of progress in producing required outputs.

Solutions

Confusion is the result of poor communication. Early project meetings explaining the project, its constraints, and goals are essential. The project manager should provide team members the opportunity to ask questions and to participate in planning the project. Clear work statements and schedules are necessary both within the project and externally to communicate to other stakeholders the status and direction of the project.

The project manager should assume that there will be confusion until clear direction is provided to all project team members. This direction should be followed up with verification that the project manager's direction is understood and will be followed.

Regular project team meetings should be held to keep everyone informed of project status and policies. In addition, the meetings will be useful to provide input to the project manager, eliminating another source of confusion.

Tips for Combating Confusion

▶ *Expect confusion at the beginning of the project.* As project manager, be prepared to address the confusion.

▶ *Make sure members of the project team and stakeholders know exactly what is expected of them,* preferably in writing.

▶ *Work with the project team and stakeholders in the scoping and planning processes,* development of the work statements and work breakdown structure, and establishment of the detailed schedules.

16

Consensus

Consensus is general agreement among the members of a given group or community, each of which exercises some discretion in decision-making and follow-up action. In the context of project management, consensus is an agreement among the interested parties—including team leaders, customers, stakeholders, and subcontractors— that a certain direction or action is acceptable to every individual in the group.

The Sin

Achieving consensus is perhaps the strongest impediment to innovative problem solving, risk management, and addressing project challenges. Since people have varying degrees of risk aversion, getting the last person to agree on a course of action means that the action is the least risky or least uncertain of all the options available. Adopting the most conservative approach—one that is acceptable to all—may result in an overly long schedule, excessively high estimated costs (see **excess**), and the **avoidance** of new methods, technologies, or processes.

Consensus is useful in planning a project; all team members must have some belief that the work can be completed within the time and funds allocated and with the technology to be used. Yet during execution, reaching consensus can waste precious time and resources. Problem solving and the emergence of new information require quick and decisive changes to the plan. These decisions must be made and implemented quickly, with limited debate, so the project can move forward in the new direction expeditiously.

Sometimes, consensus is used to avoid accountability. When a decision is made by consensus, there is no one to hold accountable: "I just went along with the group" is a common **excuse**. As Margaret Thatcher said, "To me, consensus seems to be the process of abandoning all beliefs, principles, values and policies. So it is something in which no one believes and to which no one objects."

Consensus can also erode the project manager's authority to lead the project (see **no authority**). In striving for consensus, the project manager becomes a facilitator rather than a decision-maker. The project manager forfeits the ability to make a decision based on his own risk tolerance, understanding of the issue, willingness to act, and willingness to assume the risk and be held accountable.

Nonetheless, it is important to remember that each team member is an expert in her own area, and collectively, the team has more knowledge than the project manager could possibly have. The final decision does not have to be the project manager's idea, only the best of those offered, with some rationale for its choice. As Martin Luther King said, "A genuine leader is not a searcher for consensus but a molder of consensus."

A Case of Consensus

The development of a real-time data acquisition system was planned to include five releases, or builds, with defined capabilities and scheduled release dates. The planning was done with the consensus of all the project's team leaders. Then we went into project execution. By the time we got to the third build, it was clear that this build's requirements would not be met by the planned release date. The original planning team held several meetings to address the problems we were encountering, but could not come up with workable solutions.

Once the discussion shifted from problem solving to considering which features could be deferred to later builds, the group quickly reached consensus. All agreed that the build should be released on schedule. (After all, billing milestones were at stake!)

Unfortunately, this action just pushed the most difficult work into future builds, which were already complex. As the project's progress continued to erode, it became clear that the bow wave of work ahead would mean further delays, budget overruns, and disappointed stakeholders.

In hindsight, the project manager should have reminded the team that they had reached consensus in planning the contents of the builds—and that the approach they agreed on originally was still the correct approach. The project manager should have made the decision to delay the build's release so that all the planned features could be included. This would have kept the scope of the future builds unchanged.

Danger Signs

The danger signs that consensus may be compromising your project include:

1. *A lack of leadership skills in the project manager.* A project manager should motivate others to follow her lead based on the belief that the project manager has the knowledge to set the course and that the project manager, not the project team, will be held accountable for decisions.

   A project manager who seeks consensus rather than leading is abdicating responsibility and accountability. Instead, the project manager should be ready and willing to be the only one held accountable for the entire project.

2. *A project team that insists on being involved in every decision.* Opinions are like belly buttons—everyone has one. But this does not mean they need a forum to express their opinion in any area but their own. Research shows that people know less about most subjects than they think they know, and that others think these people know more than they actually do. Accordingly, a lot of debate is required to reach consensus among a group of partially informed participants. While a project manager may not have all the knowledge, as the leader he should be prepared to interview the experts, make a decision, and assume the risk of the outcome.

Solutions

Take ownership of the project. Surround yourself with six to eight of the smartest people you can find. Ask questions, get ideas, and listen. Analyze what you have learned, address the issue, and make a decision. Require the team to follow your decision regardless of dissent and remind the team members that you are ultimately responsible for the project—and they are responsible for following your lead and direction. Your reward is based on a successful project; theirs is based on their area of expertise and following your direction.

Hold your meetings with a limited number of invitees for the purpose of asking questions and getting ideas. Avoid emailing all project members to solicit their ideas. Pick and choose your core team. Limit distribution of material to those whose thoughts you are soliciting, but don't just pick "yes" people—get a diversity of opinions.

Tips for Keeping Consensus from Destroying Your Project

▶ *As project manager, establish yourself as a leader, not a manager,* and take ownership of the outcome of the project.

▶ *Make it clear to project team members that they must be willing to follow the project manager's direction,* knowing that their success is defined by their ability to meet that direction.

17

Copying

Copying is imitating or reproducing an original.
In project management, copying most often relates
to taking credit for ideas that someone else developed.
Copying is unethical behavior on both personal
and professional levels.

The Sin

Project management has been practiced for many years, dating back to the time of the pyramids in Egypt. It became a profession in the 1950s and 1960s and has continued to grow as people recognize that projects are the key to success in organizations. Projects today are viewed as organizational assets.

As project management professionals, it is important that we use the practices that have served us and others well in the past. However, it is also important that we build on these practices and add to them so they can become best practices for others to follow.

When we adopt a practice or a theory that another person has developed, we must credit that person appropriately. We cannot adopt an idea that someone else has set forth without attribution; this conduct violates ethical standards and is detrimental to our teams and our organization. By in effect claiming that someone else's work is really our own work, we diminish the contribution of the originator and overstate our own capabilities. We **disrespect** intellectual property.

When we copy we are not acting in a truthful way, violating the codes of conduct followed by the Project Management Institute and virtually every other professional organization. Copying demonstrates that we are striving for personal gain rather than respecting our fellow practitioners.

We are all under great pressure to complete our projects on time, within budget, and according to specification. It has become all too common to look for shortcuts to meet these demands. Copying is an example of such a shortcut. The widespread use of the Internet as a resource and the availability of so much information online make it far easier than ever to engage in copying. It is also easy to engage in competitive intelligence about what is underway in other organizations and use their best practices as if they were our own work.

When we violate intellectual property considerations, we are engaging in dishonest behavior. Copying may help us complete our project on time, but in the long run others will realize that we are misrepresenting the original work of others. This can have dire consequences for our organizations, leading to possible lawsuits and litigation, not to mention the effects on our own integrity and professional reputation.

A Case of Copying

In a project procurement management class I was teaching, I asked students to prepare a job description for a procurement specialist to support a complex project. When I was reading the papers submitted in this graduate class, one of the papers sounded familiar. This was indeed the case—two students had submitted the same job description. I then did an Internet search and found they had copied word for word a job description in use by a state government. A little more research revealed that this was a relatively common practice for students submitting papers in many of my classes.

I pointed out in my classes that copying violates the university's code of conduct and is an unacceptable practice, not only in academia but also in our work as project professionals. To combat this practice, I spent hours trying to determine whether or not original work had been submitted. The ready availability of electronic books makes it very easy to copy material into many assignments. The university subsequently purchased software that detects this problem. Many universities at the master's and doctoral levels now submit project management theses and dissertations to such software before they can be approved and a degree is conferred.

Still the practice continues; no one expects to be caught.

Danger Signs

In the early stages of a project, costs are typically low because the project is just beginning and morale is high because people are excited to be part of the project. If evidence of copying is uncovered early in the project, the consequences can be destructive and costly—especially if no action is taken to address the situation. Trust then cannot form on the team, and the project's ethical standards are compromised.

If we see someone else being rewarded for work that was obviously done by others without credit, the result is low morale and a negative view of the organization. Unfortunately, if we bring the problem to the attention of others, we may be the ones considered to be the problem; we may be asked to just let it go and be told that it will not happen again. When we continue to see the practice, it may lead to reduced motivation because we feel no one cares; we may even decide to leave the organization. Either way, the result is low morale. The organization suffers because it loses key people and key intellectual property.

Solutions

Screening for copying can be done but it takes time. It also is something that we would prefer not to do as we want to trust everyone we are working with to do original work and to do their best. In today's environment, time is of the essence, and it is burdensome to have to determine whether we can trust team members.

If we do observe such behavior, we first need to check to confirm that it is copying. It is our responsibility then as project professionals to point out the behavior to the individual involved and give that person an opportunity to explain his actions. We then also need to explain why we feel it is inappropriate behavior. This is difficult to do as it takes time from our own work; moreover, it is hard to confront others and easier to walk away and avoid the problem. But if we do not take action, the behavior will continue and may have negative ramifications that affect the project and our organization. Customers and end users will lose confidence in our work and our integrity. Over the long term, our organization may not become or remain the leader in its field.

Tips for Preventing Copying on Your Project

▶ If you observe someone copying on your project, *point out the behavior and determine why it is happening.*

▶ *Lead by example* by referencing your own sources and showing the individual how you handled a similar situation in the past.

▶ If the behavior continues, *raise the issue to the next level* in an effort to effect change in the organization and continue to demonstrate in a positive way how this problem can be avoided.

▶ *Raise the topic at team meetings*—even at a kickoff meeting—as a practice to avoid throughout the project. The team could prepare a code of conduct as part of a team charter that notes that this behavior is inappropriate and will not be tolerated.

18

Cowardice

Cowardice is generally defined as lack of courage or resolution. In project management, individuals may display cowardice while fulfilling different roles throughout the project lifecycle. For example, the project manager may be reluctant, unwilling, or incapable of summoning the courage to tell the project sponsor that a proposed pet project will have disastrous consequences for the organization.

The Sin

Courage entails a basic concern to do the right thing despite the costs in situations of threat and danger. Courage enables a project manager to maintain integrity and avoid guilt and shame. It also serves as a form of moral inspiration and exemplary role-modeling to other stakeholders. Courageous project managers do not cower before superiors, do not curry favor with associates by belittling upper management, do not shrink from confronting associates with constructive project criticism, and do not cave in to pressures when the going gets tough during the project lifecycle.

In contrast, project managers who display cowardice demonstrate a loss of self-control that undermines moral virtue in themselves and others. Weakness of will is a **failure** to live up to self-imposed moral standards; it entails a willful lapse of commitment and intentions. For example, a weak-willed project manager may begin the fiscal year with a resolve to treat people on the team fairly, but within a few weeks, the project manager backslides, exhibiting **favoritism** and forgetting to be impartial in performance appraisal decisions.

The inner conflict experienced by a weak-willed project manager between ethical judgment and the will to act eventually erodes employee confidence in the sincerity of the project manager's commitments to fairness. Associates who are victimized by weak-willed project managers in turn lose respect for the project manager; even worse, they may **assume** that weak-willed, inconsistent conduct is acceptable and act accordingly. Weak-willed project managers and their teams eventually resort to making **excuses** and **scapegoating** to protect themselves from legitimate criticism.

A Case of Cowardice

I was involved with a proposed project that covered a span of three years and involved a succession of four project managers. Not one of the project managers had the courage to confront the project sponsor and address the advisability of the project in the first place.

The sponsor claimed that this cost-cutting project was important to the organization and was high on the list of things that had to be accomplished. When reports from the field indicated that recalls and rework were escalating because of substandard parts purchased in order to cut costs, the sponsor denied, trivialized, or used these reports to strengthen commitment to the pet project. Three of the four project managers were fired for being ineffective, and the fourth retained his position by never passing on the negative field reports.

It is not easy to act courageously when the sponsor is prepared to fire the project manager who does the right thing by telling truth to power. An arrogant, stubborn, and vindictive sponsor who does not listen to project feedback, whether positive or negative, must be resisted for the good of the organization and to ensure the proper allocation of resources to other feasible projects.

Danger Signs

Indicators that there is a problem with cowardice often start at the outset of a project. For example, if the project manager withholds initial critical comments regarding the feasibility of the project or its benefit to the organization as a whole, there's a problem. The project manager should have the competence and confidence of her convictions to speak freely and openly at the outset.

When the project charter is formed and ratified, it is important for the project manager to explicitly ask the project sponsor: "What happens when I bring bad news?" If the project sponsor does not want to hear any bad news, that is a danger sign that the project manager will face adverse consequences for truth-telling.

If the project manager does not pass on negative feedback regarding the project to the sponsor out of fear of repercussions, he does not have the courage to challenge the sponsor with relevant project information. The project manager must have the resolve to face and present project facts rather than cower to sponsor fiat.

If the project manager does not have the respect of the team because they realize that her cowardice is making them invest limited resources in an infeasible project advocated by a bullying sponsor, a sullen **silence** will begin to spread and team members will become more cowardly in an effort to survive in that work environment. A courageous project manager not only strengthens his own character but also cultivates the readiness of his team members to act responsibly and earns their respect.

Solutions

Cowardice is a common reason that projects drag on too long or fail. A project manager's reluctance to speak truth to power about infeasible projects is partially a function of the person and partially a function of the workplace climate. Leadership development training programs that involve top executives, middle managers, and floor supervisors—and that place a high value on personal and organizational character development—will provide a supportive context for project managers to take courageous actions. The project manager and other organizational leaders need to take advantage of training programs that focus on building leadership character.

When the problem involves the sponsor, frank discussions need to take place. A masterful project manager completes feasible projects and builds stakeholder **consensus** along the way by courageously addressing issues as they arise at all levels.

Tips for Fighting Cowardice

▶ *Speak truth to power.* If the sponsor says—or demonstrates—a reluctance to listen to negative project feedback, the project manager should find a way to communicate that feedback and act on the basis of facts rather than cower to sponsor fiat.

▶ *Encourage team members to speak truth to power.* A courageous project manager encourages team members to bring both positive and negative feedback. All team members must face facts—the sooner the better.

19

Creep

Creep generally means to move slowly, sometimes with the intent of stealth. In project management, scope creep—which can affect the budget, schedule, and overall direction of the project—doesn't necessarily move slowly nor does it remain a secret!

The Sin

Scope creep can happen during any phase of a project but it is more likely to occur during the action phases. The scope of the project can "creep" into unexpected areas, often very quickly. It can happen on small projects and big projects; the extent of the scope creep is not directly related to the size of the project.

Creep is not always negative; in certain situations it can enable the organization to tackle multiple, similar problems simultaneously, raising the project's visibility and value. For scope creep to be viewed as positive, though, it usually has to occur early on, generally in the requirements phase rather than in the action phases of a project.

Scope creep can be externally imposed (by stakeholders) or it can grow from the natural processes of working on a project (by the project manager or team members). Scope can be changed internally as the team works through the steps involved in carrying out the project. The team may discover that another issue can also be addressed using the same resources, in effect "piggybacking" on the project's original set of requirements.

Creep in a project is permissible and actually beneficial when done with deliberateness and after fully assessing project impacts. Some typical reasons for scope creep that can have negative ramifications include poorly defined or simply lacking requirements, well-defined but badly resourced project planning, or a blanket acceptance of all customer/client change requests without assessing their impacts on the project. Examples of potentially valuable and valid scope creep are unforeseen changes in the business landscape—which necessitate altering the direction, size, or outcomes/deliverables of a project to maintain its relevance—and recognition that a related business objective can be added to the project, thus meeting multiple goals by expanding the original project plan.

Regardless of the reasons for the scope creep, the project manager needs to be invested and knowledgeable to be able to manage the creep positively. Otherwise, the project may fail before it really gets off the ground.

A Case of Creep

I was working on a major IT project that needed the buy-in of a large number of stakeholders. The requirements had been vetted with each stakeholder. All the resources were in place, including some very expensive software. Ready to kick off the action phase, we brought all the stakeholders together for a meeting to make sure they were up to date on what we were doing and to present the schedule. The head of the organization attended the meeting to validate its importance to all who attended. At the end of the meeting, the CEO announced that another troubling issue for the organization had been identified that might benefit from the same software; therefore, he was changing the project to include another major IT initiative.

The two initiatives had nothing in common except that they might able to use some of the same resources, in particular the costly software. In a matter of minutes the scope of the project— its duration, cost, and direction—had changed completely. In this instance the creep was not slow and it wasn't much of a secret!

The head of the organization had the authority to make such a decision, and the project manager and his team had to find a way to make it work. Needless to say, the project team immediately went to work to make changes in just about every aspect of the original plan.

Danger Sign

A sure sign that scope creep is taking place is when you find yourself or your team members saying, "How are we ever going to accomplish all this?"

Solutions

The project manager should review "out of scope" items as frequently as the in-scope items added to the project. The out-of-scope list should be reviewed at least every six weeks. Consider, though, that they must be important issues or they wouldn't have come up in the first place.

Depending on the size and complexity of the project, the project manager should have a change control process in place to manage scope creep issues. Ideally, this process should be a documented project artifact that is explained to project members and client stakeholders in advance of a project change request. This document should define the criteria and timing for acceptable project changes, as well as the manner in which these scope changes will be handled. Formalizing the process involved in adopting project scope changes ensures that the project manager is fully considering and managing all necessary project details—such as adjusting resources and timelines.

Tips for Keeping Creep from Destroying Your Project

▶ *Accept it.* No project starts on day one of an issue. You are never starting a project completely fresh. Acknowledge and accept that pre-existing issues can affect any stage of the project.

▶ *Stay fluid.* Scope creep happens and you have to be flexible enough to adjust your expectations and your plans.

▶ *Document.* Every change in the scope of the project should be documented.

▶ *Recognize and deal with scope changes.* Make sure you're still on track to meet the project's goals and objectives (or consider the need to revise them) rather than just "going with the flow."

▶ *Manage expectations.* As changes occur, keep the stakeholders and sponsors informed of their impact.

▶ *Be sensitive to morale issues.* When creep takes over, team members can start to believe that the project will never end. The project manager should take the time to redefine success for each member of the team.

▶ *Stay in control.* Always remember that your primary job is to manage the project, not just hold back **chaos**.

20

Democracy

Democracy is a form of government in which the supreme power is vested in the people and exercised directly by them or by their elected agents under a free electoral system. In project management, democracy has to do with how decisions are made on the project team. Generally, you want people on the project to contribute their ideas without diluting the project manager's responsibility or leadership.

The Sin

Democracy is fairly common in project management. Engaging everyone on the project team can be very effective in gaining their commitment. When everyone's voice is heard, the team benefits from a diversity of opinions and is often able to come up with innovative solutions to problems. However, the democratic process of voting entails the risk of making the wrong decision because not everyone sees the project in its entirety. The project manager has the higher level view of how all the pieces fit together.

Democracy also raises the issue of the "fair" way to make a decision. For example, if the makeup of the project team is heavily skewed toward sales and only one person represents finance, should the finance representative's vote count for more? For certain types of decisions but not others?

Democracy is most destructive at the stage in a project when complex decisions must be made. Project teams can usually agree on the easy decisions that are clear-cut, don't involve much controversy, or have limited options.

A Case of Democracy

I was involved with a project that covered a 12-month planning period prior to the event. I had worked on projects like this before and had the advantage of several after-action reviews that had been completed on predecessor projects. The event was the same as we had planned in the past, the location was the same, and many of the project team members were veterans of prior projects. The one new ingredient was the project manager. On the surface, he seemed to be very qualified, with the right skills and experience to manage the project. Unfortunately, he just did not want to make decisions.

From the start, the team would meet to discuss certain aspects of the project; after everyone had their say, we would vote on what route to take. Initially, this path was promising because the project team members all felt they had ownership in the direction of the project. However, on the first difficult decision we faced, the project team could not reach **consensus** and discussions ended in a stalemate. We returned to discuss and negotiate the issue several times but were not able to resolve differences, make a decision, and move forward.

Our inability to reach consensus and the project manager's inability to make a decision delayed the project several weeks; successor tasks that were dependent on us resolving our differences were also delayed. Teamwork suffered as factions started to **blame** each other for holding up the decision. Finally, when it became apparent that the project was mired in stalemate and the project manager was unwilling to make a decision, he was replaced and the project was able to move forward.

Danger Sign

An early danger sign of democracy on a project is the project manager's tendency to defer to the wishes of the project team. It is the project manager's job to solicit all relevant points of view on an issue and then make the best decision in terms of the overall project goal.

Solutions

The choice of a project manager is critical. The project team members are usually specialists in their area or field; the project manager must have a 360-degree view of the project and be able to make informed decisions. The project manager has to be decisive and make the right decisions at the right time. Key ingredients are having an intellectual curiosity that leads to asking the right questions and being an active listener when the response is given.

Tips for Managing Democracy

▶ *Consider leadership skills* when selecting a project manager.

▶ *Consult your team* for information and then, as project manager, make the best decision.

▶ *Engage the team* to support the decisions you have made.

21

Despair

Despair is the loss of **hope** or confidence, a state of hopelessness. In project management, despair can be experienced when a project is poorly planned or is not proceeding according to plan and there seems to be no hope for improvement.

The Sin

In organizations with little project experience or **immature** project management practices, despair is common. The project manager can feel despair when faced with obviously unrealistic expectations or baselines on a project, or when a previous project manager planned the project poorly. Insufficient resources, lack of organizational attention, or reluctance to change conditions in a failing project (see **failure**) can also cause despair for a project manager.

It is all too easy for despair to lead to a "victim mind-set" on the part of the project manager. This outlook will inevitably infect the entire team and its efforts.

A Case of Despair

The goal of any project is to deliver a unique product, service, or result. New product development is an example of a project type that consistently falls prey to despair. I was involved in the startup of a new product (and company) that had a simple-sounding, two-part business plan: (1) develop the product and (2) market the product.

Little formal planning was devoted to the effort; the project essentially took the form of a near-obsessive "just do it" venture. The product development phase went pretty well, yielding a well-reviewed innovation with wide market potential. By the time the market launch was undertaken, though, almost no financial resources were left. As it became obvious that the product was not going to take off, and that the entire project was plagued by **magical thinking**, severe despair set in for the entire team.

In the end, the company failed, the employees left, the investment was lost, and thousands of dollars spent on the finished product were wasted. The owners of the company were so demoralized that they gave up on the entrepreneurial lifestyle (despite previous successful startups) and took jobs with other organizations.

Danger Signs

Despair is most destructive and costly during the execution, monitoring, and controlling stages of a project, when the disparity between the plan and performance can become so broad and obvious that all hope of success is lost. Expenditures are high and the potential loss of money, time, and reputation can overwhelm the project manager and the team. To head off despair before it takes an irreversible toll on the project, the project manager and team should watch out for:

▶ Poorly thought-out justification or business cases

▶ Lack of or inadequate project charter

▶ Unrealistic goals and expectations

▶ Insufficient project plans.

Solutions

To avoid reaching a point of despair in your project, always objectively assess any effort you are assigned to manage. It will help to document your concerns about shortcomings and present them in a professional manner to the organization's decision-makers. If you envision a problem or **barriers**, offer written, rational alternatives to problem situations and recommend and defend your best options. And, of course, consistently apply project management best practices and provide leadership to the team—no matter the probable outcome.

Tips for Combating Despair

▶ *Do not lose sight of the basic principles of good planning* even when project enthusiasm and morale are soaring.

▶ *Recognize the need to objectively examine a project early* and be willing to recommend "pulling the plug" if the required resources are not available.

▶ *Accept the fact that some projects will fail*—and that life and careers go on.

22

Deviation

Deviation is a departure from a standard or norm, an abnormality. In project management, deviation is the departure from the basic rules of project management when confronted with a difficult or stressful situation.

The Sin

Each project manager is different. A less experienced project manager may adhere to basic, established best practices and internal organizational procedures. A more experienced project manager may rely on a combination of basic best practices, trial-and-error, and wizened judgment. Regardless, all project managers can and should list a handful of basic project management principles that they firmly believe are applicable to their management of projects—and they should not deviate from those principles.

Deviation is pervasive in project management, and it just might be the #1 reason for project **failure**. Studies by Gartner, Forrester

Research, and the Standish Group have determined that the top reasons for project failure have remained fairly constant for a decade or two, including unclear requirements, a lack of user involvement, and inadequate executive support. A simpler notion is that projects typically fail because project managers deviate from the basics of project management.

A Case of Not Deviating

A story about one of the greatest project managers of all time illustrates this hypothesis. Margot Morrell and Stephanie Capparell tell the story of Ernest Shackleton in their book, *Shackleton's Way*:

> From 1914 to 1916, Ernest Shackleton and his men survived the wreck of their ship *Endurance*, in the crushing Antarctic ice, stranded twelve hundred miles from civilization with no means of communication and no hope for rescue. The temperatures were so low the men could hear water freeze. They subsisted on a diet of penguins, dogs, and seals. And when the ice began to break up, Shackleton set out to save them all on his heroic eight-hundred-mile trip across the frigid South Atlantic—in little more than a rowboat. Unlike other polar expeditions, every man survived—not only in good health, but also in good spirits—all due to the leadership of Shackleton.[1]

What did Shackleton do to achieve this spectacular project success? Did he adhere to a planned schedule or stick to a particular budget? Did he even fulfill the original goal of the project: to be the first to traverse Antarctica via the South Pole? Not at all. His project took several times longer than planned, it was enormously over-budget, and he never even set foot on Antarctica.

---

1. Margot Morrell and Stephanie Capparell, *Shackleton's Way: Leadership Lessons from the Great Antarctic Explorer* (London: Penguin Books, Ltd., 2002).

Despite these circumstances, Shackleton ultimately succeeded because he had the discipline not to deviate from the basics. For him, the basics included constant communication with his men, not only en masse but also one-on-one. This communication occurred in daily standup meetings and in private discussions when he visited each man every day. He asked how each member of the expedition was doing, how they felt, what they thought, and what they needed. He did this when their ship was being crushed by pack ice, when they were drifting in lifeboats, and when they were stranded on a barren pile of rocks in the middle of nowhere.

He discussed the objectives of the expedition, the conditions he and his men were in, and the need to constantly refine, adjust, and eventually change the expedition's requirements. Together, Shackleton and his men changed the expedition's goal from exploration to survival. By adhering to the discipline of communication, Shackleton and his men developed a culture and environment where even in the harshest, most life-threatening conditions, his men wrote in their diaries that it was the best time of their lives.

Shackleton was an experienced and knowledgeable exploration project manager: He had led several previous expeditions and he had studied other exploration project managers. Using this knowledge and experience, he systematically developed a list of project management basics from which he would not—and did not—deviate.

Danger Signs

Recognition and screening require a substantial amount of objectivity—to examine the course of a project and assess it according to a list of relevant basics developed by an experienced project manager. In addition to a quick assessment of the project against this list, the project manager should periodically probe team members to determine their propensity to stick to or deviate from the basics. For example, if a team member responds to a request to provide cost estimates without including caveats and assumptions about project scope and requirements, this could mean the team member might be inclined to deviate from the basics.

Lessons Learned

In his book, *Alpha Project Managers: What The Top 2% Know That Everyone Else Does Not,* Andy Crowe provides extraordinary insight into what top-performing project managers know and do that sets them apart. Based on a survey of 5,000 project managers and stakeholders, the study focuses on identifying the best—or "Alpha"—project managers and determining why they are successful by interviewing their team members, customers, and managers.[2]

The differences between Alpha and non-Alpha project managers are revealing. For example, although both Alphas and non-Alphas equally understand the importance of planning, Alphas typically dedicate double the project time to actual planning. Similarly, although both Alphas and non-Alphas equally understand the value of communication, Alphas are more effective communicators simply because they invest more effort in communications.

---

2. Andy Crowe, *Alpha Project Managers: What The Top 2% Know That Everyone Else Does Not* (Kennesaw, Georgia: Velociteach, 2006).

Although virtually all project managers in Crowe's study could clearly identify the importance of planning and communicating, Alphas had the discipline to actually follow through with those activities to the degree necessary. Like Shackleton, Alphas do more than acknowledge the basics; they adhere to the basics without deviating.

Of course, adhering to the basics is easier said than done—it requires courage, backbone, fortitude, and resilience. The modern-day project management guru Neal Whitten writes in his book, *No-Nonsense Advice for Successful Projects*: "It is my experience that project managers are not willing to make the tough and unpopular project-related decisions (see **popularity**), even though their instincts warn them that they are not taking the most effective action."[3] To make tough and unpopular decisions, and to be successful, project managers have to form what highly regarded business expert Jim Collins describes as "an absolutely iron will."[4]

Tips for Keeping Deviation from Derailing Your Project

▶ *Systematically develop a list of project management basics* and do not deviate from these basics on your project.

▶ *Periodically probe team members* to determine their propensity to stick to or deviate from the basics.

▶ *Adhere to the basics* even when doing so requires making tough and unpopular decisions.

---

3. Neal Whitten, *Neal Whitten's No-Nonsense Advice for Successful Projects* (Vienna, VA: Management Concepts, 2005), p. 42.

4. Jim Collins, *Good to Great: Why Some Companies Make the Leap . . . and Others Don't* (New York: HarperCollins, 2001), p. 271.

23

Dispassion

Dispassion is a state or quality of being unemotional or emotionally uninvolved. In projects, dispassion manifests itself as a lack of caring about the overall process, documentation, team facilitation, and leadership.

The Sin

A project manager or team member without passion fosters apathy, low team morale, and poor project performance. Fortunately, dispassion is becoming less of an issue as project management is increasingly seen as a distinct career path that requires a particular, unique set of skills.

Dispassion in projects is typically exhibited by "accidental" project managers—team members promoted into project management without the requisite skill set to be successful. This leads to frustration for the project manager and, eventually, to detachment and dispassion.

Especially in technical realms, project management is a logical career progression milestone. Unfortunately, simply being a good performer and great coder, engineer, or tester does not necessarily translate into being a good (or even adequate) project manager.

A Case of Dispassion

I was brought into a very large IT project to perform a project assessment one month prior to the go-live application date. The entire project team was captive in a "focus" room where they were all working hard to ensure that the application would be deployed as promised. (The application delivery was already two years late and several million dollars over budget.)

When I found the project manager, he was seated in the middle of the room with his head buried in lines of code. He was actually coding the application. He was clearly not facilitating the process or communicating with key stakeholders. This project manager had failed to make the transition to project leader, falling back into the familiar and comfortable world of application developer. His project management role became a burden rather than a challenge for him and he ultimately lost his passion for the project's performance.

Reviewing the history of the project, it became clear that dispassion was present from the very first project manager, who was apparently placed in the position without the requisite training, skill, and motivation to perform the duties. The result of this initial dispassion was a project that was severely late and over budget—conditions that fostered dispassion in the next project manager.

Danger Signs

Some of the early warning signs of dispassion are project managers not requiring adherence to task dates, team members delivering late, and disinterested stakeholders. Because of the subtlety of the symptoms, it is difficult to screen for dispassion. Behaviors and actions are the best way to determine if team members are experiencing dispassion. For example, someone on the team may spend more time performing in a role for which he has more passion and interest than the role he is supposed to be performing on your project.

While dispassion can be destructive and costly in each stage of a project, the execution stage is where it has the most costly and destructive impacts. Lack of interest often results in frequent rework and defects. A close second is in the planning stage. If a project manager or team is dispassionate in the planning stage, it's a sure bet that incomplete plans will lead to substandard execution.

Solutions

As project manager, take ownership of what you do. Consider each project you are leading as your personal business. Own it and run it as such. Take whatever steps are necessary to involve your team from the beginning to help grow their ownership. Offer your team opportunities for decision-making on the project, starting small and progressing to moderately large decisions. Showing this type of confidence in your team members will go a long way toward helping them develop a strong sense of ownership and thus guard against dispassion.

Tips for Countering Dispassion

▶ *Ensure that people are assigned to work on tasks for which they're prepared and they enjoy.* If your resources are not actively engaged in your project, chances are that it will fail.

▶ *Have frequent personal dialog with your team members individually.* People will respond much better to a leader when they sense they are truly cared for and valued.

▶ *Sell the project vision to your team.* When team members believe strongly in a cause, they will display more passion in performing. Your job is to sell that vision and inspire passion.

▶ *Be actively involved personally in your project.* Without the project manager's active involvement, **failure** is almost certain.

24

Disrespect

Disrespect is the condition of having or showing no respect or even courteous regard for others. In project management, individuals and teams fulfilling different roles throughout the project lifecycle may display disrespect. For example, project managers may show disrespect for their internal or external project stakeholders or for the team operating procedures to which they committed in the project charter.

The Sin

Respect entails being attentive to and taking seriously the concerns, needs, and relationship demands of project stakeholders and abiding by the operational processes agreed to in the project charter. Respect ensures that the project manager has a good handle on what is going on regarding the project and is aware of stakeholder concerns. Respect ensures that project stakeholders know their concerns are being identified, prioritized, and taken seriously—not ignored or neglected. Project managers exhibit disrespect when they are indifferent to project stakeholder concerns (regardless of their proximity, urgency, or power), are **careless** about adhering to project charter processes, and are rude toward project stakeholders who express concerns.

A Case of Disrespect

An egregious case of disrespect was when financial project managers originated and resold subprime mortgages to domestic and global buyers who were unaware of the nature and extent of the risks embedded in their original loans and securitized debt obligations (which ratings agencies evaluated as "AAA"). At the micro-level, the project managers' disrespect for borrower qualifying standards enabled unqualified borrowers to take on subprime mortgages that they would likely default on in the future. At the macro level, the project managers at ratings agencies disrespected the needs of domestic and global consumers for objective ratings of financial products when they rated financial products AAA to accelerate agency revenue. The cumulative impact of this multilevel process of project manager disrespect led to both domestic and global credit crises.

It is not easy for project managers to act respectfully to other project stakeholders in the face of private sector pressures for short-term profits and public sector pressures for votes in the next election. However, those project managers in banks, mortgage lending firms, and ratings agencies who avoided the project sin of disrespect protected their firms from bankruptcy, lawsuits, and loss of reputation. The project managers who led their solvent financial institutions by bypassing "bad money" options are now able to operate their firms without government bailouts and taxpayer funds—and with their reputations intact for prudently respecting stakeholder long-term interests.

Danger Signs

If the project manager ignores or neglects the concerns of internal and external project stakeholders at the outset of a project, this is a danger sign that the scope of the project is likely too narrow and therefore will encounter resistance from disrespected stakeholders. The respectful project manager should identify and be prepared to seriously engage the concerns of all relevant project stakeholders.

If the project manager ignores or unilaterally violates the operating processes agreed to in the project charter, this is a danger sign that the project manager's promise to respect past and future contractual processes cannot be trusted. A pattern of disrespecting project charter processes will influence project team members to do likewise. The net result will be that neither the project manager nor the project team will attract repeat sponsors, partners, or clients because no other project stakeholder will want to risk being treated with disrespect.

If the project manager responds rudely or vindictively to project stakeholders who voice concerns about the project, this is a danger sign that constructive, corrective feedback from project partners will be disrespected. Respectful project managers do not treat project stakeholders with contempt or disrespect them by bullying or intimidating them for voicing their concerns.

Solutions

Disrespect is a common reason that projects fail or are abandoned. A project manager's disrespect for project stakeholder relationships or project charter processes is partially a function of the person and partially a function of the workplace culture. Leadership development training programs for project managers that focus on the importance of demonstrating respect for stakeholder relationships and charter processes will provide a supportive context to legitimize and reinforce respectful attitudes and actions. The project manager and other organizational leaders need to take advantage of such training programs so that respectful regard for project stakeholder relationships and processes becomes a strong norm in the work culture.

When the problem involves project team members, the project manager must intervene, listen to the concerns of diverse team members, facilitate resolutions based on common values, and maintain a culture of respectful agreement or disagreement within the team. A respectful project manager recognizes, listens to, and responds to project stakeholder concerns and abides by the operational processes committed to in the project charter. A mature, competent project manager earns the respect of stakeholders by demonstrating respectful regard for others and charter **promises**.

Tips for Addressing Disrespect

▶ *Actively solicit, listen to, and respond to stakeholder concerns.* If the project manager shows respect for project stakeholder relationships by being attentive to their concerns on a regular basis and in an organized manner, the stakeholders are more likely to reciprocate with thoughtful feedback and cooperative contributions.

▶ *Demonstrate respect for project charter operating processes.* A respectful project manager abides by the operating processes committed to in the project charter and thereby sets an important example for project team members.

25

Dysfunction

Dysfunction is generally defined as a **failure** to function in an expected or complete manner. Dysfunction occurs in project management when an individual or group does not or cannot perform its role properly, resulting in abnormal project operations.

The Sin

Projects are done for, by, and with people, making the social structure within the project itself, and in the related environment, an important source of potential dysfunction. In its simplest form, project management is having the right people doing the right thing at the right time for the right reason. This may sound elementary, but in actuality, for all but the simplest of projects, achieving this state can be quite challenging. Much of the challenge arises from the many sources of potential dysfunction in projects.

Three key sources of dysfunction in projects are:

1. *Mismanagement in the organization*—a lack of understanding or poor implementation of basic management principles

not just in the project, but also in the organization owning the project.

2. *Misunderstanding of the goals or objectives of the project*—inadequate or improper definition, planning, execution, or control of the project to achieve its intent.

3. **Misalignment** *of the people involved*—not understanding who is doing what, how they are doing it, and when. Dysfunction can result from incorrect understanding of the work, inability to do the work, or perhaps unwillingness to do the work.

Dysfunction will occur when the project team does not understand the goals and objectives of the project, or does not have adequate resources and a realistic schedule to accomplish them.

A Case of Dysfunction

NASA is respected for its ability to accomplish difficult and highly complex projects, yet is occasionally subject to dysfunction in its project management. One example is the Mars Climate Orbiter, designed to function as an interplanetary weather satellite in NASA's Mars Surveyor program. Using a "faster, better, cheaper" project approach, the Mars Climate Orbiter was launched on December 11, 1998, from Cape Canaveral in Florida to arrive at Mars in December 1999. On September 23, 1999, the spacecraft was lost while entering the Martian atmosphere on a trajectory that was too low to achieve its intended orbit. According to the investigative team, the root cause of the loss of the spacecraft was a failed translation between English units and metric units used in the ground-based, navigation-related mission software.

NASA lost the development costs of the orbiter ($189 million), the launch vehicle, and all the launch expenses, plus the costs for the review, analysis, and reporting of the failure. Perhaps a greater cost was the embarrassment within NASA and the Jet Propulsion Laboratory, which managed the project, over losing a satellite project because of such an obvious mistake.

What was involved in the dysfunction leading up to this failure from the premier U.S. project management organization? Dysfunction in this project occurred in all three key areas.

First, management failed to clearly define and implement the faster-better-cheaper approach to projects in NASA, and they accepted a less-than-realistic budget for the project. This led to **conflict** between the project goals and the faster-better-cheaper approach. This conflict in turn created the second dysfunction, misunderstanding of the goals and objectives of the project. More attention was focused on meeting cost and schedule requirements than on the risks involved. At the heart of the orbiter loss was the final dysfunction, misalignment of the people involved. Communications channels were too informal, the small mission navigation team was overextended, peer review by independent experts was not conducted, and personnel were not sufficiently trained in areas related to the operation of the mission and its detailed navigational characteristics. Both poor project leadership and a lack of discipline in problem identification on the project led to these dysfunctions.

Everyone involved in a project has a duty to point out dysfunction where they see it. Dysfunction due to misalignment of the people involved in the Mars Orbiter project must have been recognized by at least those who felt misaligned, including the navigation team members who were overextended and did not receive the necessary peer review. Many of the contributing causes of the loss of the Mars Orbiter might have been ameliorated if these problems had been identified and brought to the attention of NASA management.

Solutions

To manage projects successfully in your organization, it is not enough to simply identify and fund those projects. Management is responsible for ensuring that all project teams understand both the organization's and their project's goals and objectives—and have adequate resources and a realistic schedule for accomplishing them. All projects are, in the end, management's projects.

The project manager is responsible for ensuring that the project team clearly understands the goals and objectives of the project. After identifying what is needed to meet project goals and objectives, and devising the plan for how to achieve them, the project team must realistically identify the resources needed and determine how long the project will take given these resources.

If the resources to complete the project are inadequate to meet the plan within the required time frame, the project manager must make that inadequacy known to organizational management. Management may have flexibility, or constraints, not known to the project manager.

If management has some flexibility, perhaps a reduced scope, additional resources, or an extended schedule is possible. If management has constraints, perhaps the project is a poor choice to undertake at this time and it can be canceled or postponed before it begins. The project manager is expected to complete the project she is assigned, but cannot be expected to work miracles with unclear goals, insufficient resources, or unrealistic time to accomplish the work involved.

Tips for Keeping Dysfunction from Destroying Your Project

▶ *Clarify the expected results* of the project and adequately define its goals and objectives.

▶ *Gain the strong support* of a project sponsor.

▶ *Understand the project goals* and objectives.

▶ *Ensure that project team members are willing and able* to do the necessary work.

26

Ego

Ego means the self as distinguished from others; the term usually connotes an exaggerated sense of self-importance, conceit, boastfulness, or selfishness, or an excessive and objectionable reference to oneself in conversation or writing. In project management, ego typically motivates strong-willed team members who believe they know the best way to do things and are reluctant to listen to others.

The Sin

Ego is especially prevalent in industries that equate knowledge with power. Individuals who have repeatedly been successful conducting tasks their own way without considering input from others are at risk of letting their egos rule their decisions.

Environments that reward individual performance rather than team performance or project success encourage self-centeredness. Many organizations reward "winners" (real or perceived) who, through their own will and determination, work at a problem persistently until they achieve success. Unfortunately, the success of these "winners" is often interpreted as a personal triumph even though it is rarely achieved without the help of others.

Ego can manifest itself in many behaviors, including those exhibited by individuals who:

▶ Take more credit for project outcomes than they deserve

▶ Are reluctant to change a course of action once they have made a decision

▶ Are unwilling to admit or even consider the possibility that a mistake or error has occurred

▶ When challenged, respond with negative behaviors, outbursts, or anger

▶ Interpret any criticism, no matter how objective and regardless of its delivery, as a personal attack

▶ Relish the misfortune of others, especially when the misfortune personally benefits them or happens to a perceived opponent or adversary

▶ Feel too busy to provide support or assistance to others without inconveniencing themselves.

In a broader sense, ego manifests itself in a lack of communication, information-sharing, openness, and trust, and by delayed resolutions or decisions.

A Case of Ego Gone Awry

A historical example of ego at work is General Douglas MacArthur's actions during the Korean War. Following his success in the Pacific theatre during World War II and early victories in Korea, MacArthur's political stature—and his ego—rose steadily.

His view of himself and his abilities began to drive his decision-making.

According to several military historians, MacArthur did not like hearing bad news. Instead, he surrounded himself with advisors and staff who would tell him what he wanted to hear or who would provide information to support a position he had already taken. As a result, MacArthur was rarely provided the information necessary to make intelligent decisions in Korea; when appropriate information was provided, he often ignored it.

Propelled by his ego, MacArthur insisted he knew the strength of the North Korean and Chinese armies and the willingness of the Soviet Union to enter the conflict, when in fact his perceptions were wrong. As a result, the Korean War became what some consider the most significant failed project in history. MacArthur's ego also prevented him from ever acknowledging any personal responsibility for U.S. failures during the conflict. Instead, he **blamed** all the other stakeholders, including China, his officers and staff, the U.S. Congress, and President Harry Truman.

The Costs of Ego

Ego has both tangible and intangible costs. Tangible costs include waste, scrap, and rework that result from stubbornness or an unwillingness to consider various options and perspectives. When a project manager's overbearing ego makes stakeholders reluctant to present particular information, he becomes more likely to make decisions that cause schedule delays, cost overruns, and overall dissatisfaction with project deliverables. As a result, customers may take their business elsewhere. The intangible costs of ego include fear, hostility, and low morale.

Danger Signs

Over the long term, egos are difficult to hide. Egocentric people seek out power and **politics**. How actively does someone try to place herself in positions of leadership? Are these tendencies followed for the sake of the team or organization, or is the underlying purpose to achieve personal gain? Does the individual surround himself with "yes men"?

Human resource experts warn hiring managers to be cautious of individuals who constantly use the words "I" and "me" in an interview. Managers are also alerted to be wary of those who respond to feedback or critical analysis by rationalizing their behavior, dismissing the comments out of hand, or becoming hostile.

Tips for Preventing Ego from Destroying Your Project

▶ *Strive to help others succeed.*

▶ *Establish a relationship with someone you trust* who is not afraid to communicate honestly about both good and bad project conditions.

▶ *When communicating with an egocentric person, present facts rather than opinions.* This might require some extra research and documentation, but facts will be more difficult for an egocentric person to refute stubbornly.

▶ *Seek out and encourage the opinions and perspectives of others,* even if they are not your strongest allies.

27

Excess

Excess is surpassing usual, proper, or specified limits, or exhibiting undue or immoderate indulgence. In project management, excess is the failure to be realistic in planning a project. Typically, excess means that one or more stakeholders expect that the work of the project—the scope—is out of line with the schedule and available resources, exhibiting undue indulgence or, in other words, wishful thinking.

The Sin

I am reminded of my first trip to a cafeteria with my great aunt and uncle when I was eight years old. It seemed to be a gastronomical wonderland! Moving through the serving line, I loaded my tray with all sorts of goodies. When my great aunt commented, "Your eyes are bigger than your stomach," I was puzzled by her understanding of anatomy. Graciously, they paid for the entire bounty I had collected and withheld comments about my eating only a small portion of my lunch.

When similar indulgence takes place on projects, the stakes are dramatically higher. We engage in excess when we expect more than the project can realistically deliver . . . when our eyes are bigger than what the project can stomach.

As a result of the interdependent nature of scope and quality, schedule, and resources, the sin of excess has a range of manifestations on a project. When planning is realistic, a project is more likely to inspire confidence from the start. However, if the planning process is governed by wishful thinking, or excess, rather than realism, a host of project troubles will surely result.

Excess also places pressure on truth and integrity. When excess is prevalent, the project may exist in two parallel universes. In the "public" version, everything is proceeding according to plan. The other version is the reality, the truth. To bring the two universes closer, some team members may feel compelled to cut corners on quality (see **shoddy quality**).

A Case of Excess

Consider the "Big Dig" project in Boston, officially known as the Central Artery/Tunnel project. This massive undertaking, the largest highway project in U.S. history, was designed to relieve perennial traffic congestion in downtown Boston. The centerpiece of the project, and its namesake, was a tunnel through the heart of the downtown area.

The effects of excess on this project were so substantial and far-reaching that it would perhaps be easier to make a list of what was *not* affected. Nevertheless, the short list of negative effects includes:

▶ *Severe cost overruns.* The original, inflation-adjusted budget was $6 billion, while the final cost was $22 billion.

- *Interest.* Of the $22 billion final cost, the cost of interest alone was $7 billion, much of which is attributable to the project's **lateness**.

- *Schedule.* Opinions vary, but the project was completed five to nine years late.

- *Fines.* The governing authority charged contractors more than $100 million in fines.

- *Fatality.* Part of the tunnel collapsed, killing a member of the public.

- *Indictments.* Associated with the fatality, indictments were issued.

- *Structural integrity.* Concerns persist about the engineering integrity of the completed tunnel, particularly leaks and structural problems, with fears of future collapses.

- *Closures.* The structural integrity issues have led to the need for inspections and repairs, causing road closures and traffic problems.

- *Morale.* The public, including taxpayers, lost significant confidence in the project and became exceedingly cynical: The Big Dig became "yet *another* government blunder."

All these negative effects share the same root causes: an excess of optimism, or wishful thinking, and the failure to use an appropriate model to plan and manage the project.

Danger Signs

The most effective way to recognize the sin of excess is to look for excessive optimism that borders on fantasy (see **magical** thinking). This can be accomplished by anonymously polling a number of knowledgeable, yet independent people. One method would be to have each person polled offer a confidence level (0–100 percent) that the project will be successful given the baseline scope, schedule, and resources. It should be a clear danger sign when the aggregate answers trend below 90 percent.

Solutions

What can be learned from the Big Dig? First, avoid fantasy in planning. This was an off-the chart extensive project that involved many unknowns and new techniques. It was inevitable that there would be surprises. The solution is to use a planning and management model for such a project that accommodates its novelty, ambiguity, and complexity.

Second, as an enormous governmental project, there were many opportunities for **mismanagement**. One of the root causes of the mismanagement was that the controlling governmental authority essentially turned over project management to a private consulting firm. The justification for this arrangement was that the authority lacked experience in managing a project of this magnitude. As a result, the public controls over the project were exceedingly weak.

So many characteristics of this project screamed that there would be trouble long before ground was broken. A governmental project of this size should have been divided into smaller pieces with far more transparency and oversight. There should have been additional experimentation and phasing of work. All participants should have realized that this type of novel, complex project would be far more difficult and complicated than was indicated in the plan.

Tips for Avoiding Excess

▶ Critically evaluate each element of the scope of work during the planning process.

▶ Separate "needs" from "wants." Be willing to ruthlessly exclude those elements of the scope that are nice to have but are not essential to the mission of the project.

▶ Identify and adhere to the critical success factors for the project.

▶ Be wary of scope elements that have never been attempted before or those that can succeed only if multiple factors work together perfectly.

▶ Divide the overall scope into manageable pieces. A piece is manageable only when there is a high level of confidence that it can be achieved according to plan.

▶ Have regular project review meetings and be willing to cut back on scope if it becomes apparent that the project is getting out of control.

▶ Above all, emphasize that honesty and realism must be the cornerstones of project communication.

28

Exclusion

Exclusion is preventing or restricting participation, consideration, or inclusion. The term is usually applied to people, for example, of certain races, religions, or sexual preferences. In project management, exclusion occurs when a project manager exhibits a total focus on her own project, to the detriment of other projects or other work of the organization.

The Sin

Exclusion is far more common in project management than we would like to believe because it is usually hidden from public view. For example, all materials required on a project are requisitioned at the beginning of the project and locked up so they cannot be "stolen" by other, perhaps more critical, projects, even if they will not be required on the current project for a considerable time. The same behavior can be observed with human resources, when a specialty skill is assigned some kind of work just to keep the person tied to the project until all specialty tasks have been completed. All other projects are excluded from sharing this resource.

Even when it is obvious that certain project managers are hoarding resources, corrective action is seldom taken. Instead, most organizations reward individual project managers for completing their individual assignments rather than for assisting the entire organization in achieving its goals.

An organization that encourages employees to focus on their individual performance by allowing exclusionary behavior is destroying or severely hampering any team spirit that provides job satisfaction and commitment. This environment is built, over time, at untold cost and lost opportunities. Some good, potentially great, employees will leave organizations that promote or permit exclusionary behavior. In addition, the organization, if it advances at all, does so in fits and starts, keeping progress intermittent and unpredictable.

Excluding other projects, departments, or units by hoarding resources typically benefits only the manager practicing the exclusion. We all know of instances where a project manager could have lent resources to another, more critical, area and refused to do so if there was any chance that his project might not get the resources back in time to proceed in accordance with the baseline schedule. In this case, the cost to the organization came from the projects that were unable to acquire the resources they desperately needed to make progress. Environments in which exclusion is tolerated typically suffer from poor morale, retaliation, and an "every person for themselves" attitude that severely limits an organization's ability to make coordinated progress toward its goals.

A Case of Exclusion

For the project manager practicing exclusion, results are mixed. For example, excluding a contrarian's advice that something is not right might cause a minor problem to escalate into a huge problem. NASA ignored warnings from engineers not to launch the *Challenger* in January 1986, and the resulting disaster cost lives and set the U.S. space program back a number of years. Besides the tragic loss of life, the *Challenger* disaster was a public relations nightmare for NASA and most likely cost the agency millions of dollars of congressional support. In addition to the cost of wasting many months trying to unravel how the disaster could have occurred, morale and NASA employee retention suffered.

Danger Signs

The "tone at the top," which greatly influences company culture, is critical in properly aligning all projects to achieve organizational goals. Company "hero" culture is the first indication that managers are not inclined to work together and a bunker mentality can be expected. Certain managers are always successful because they have learned to game the system by hoarding resources (people as well as equipment and other materials) or getting what they need by schmoozing resource managers or screaming louder than other managers.

Rewarding individual project managers, rather than the project team, for bringing in a project on time, or punishing managers for failing to do so, is an indication that an exclusionary environment is tolerated. Constantly changing project priorities is also a signal that priorities may be set without sufficient insight into what is best for the organization.

Ignoring risk, as well as contrarian advice, is another indication that top executives may not be making thoughtful decisions. The best ways to identify an exclusionary environment is by conducting some due diligence of the organization and its reputation, or by observing how project priorities are established whenever there is contention for resources.

Solutions

Competition and communication today are such that authoritarian management will not be able to compete with a team of employees all working toward the same goals. No matter how brilliant an individual or small group of individuals might be, they cannot outperform committed and smart employees working together to improve the organization.

Exclusion is permitted in organizations that reward only individual effort and results, regardless of what they say about "team players." Frequently, competition inside this type of firm is as great as, or greater than, competition with outsiders.

To minimize or eliminate exclusion, an organization must hire good employees and evaluate them based on their contribution to the group effort. In addition, priorities must be established from the top levels of the organization (every project cannot be number one!) so that everyone knows where exceptional effort should be applied.

One way or another, priorities should be set based on thoughtful logic and not determined by individuals on the spur of the moment.

Tips for Protecting against Exclusion

▶ *Establish clear project priorities.*

▶ *Use a project portfolio approach.*

▶ *Weight project team/organization performance equally with individual performance.*

▶ *Level work required* so you do not constantly overload resources.

▶ *Expect and reward behavior that benefits the organization.*

▶ *Honor contrarians* (who frequently have a legitimate concern, even it they do not always express themselves clearly).

29

Excuses

Making **excuses** is making an apology for, trying to remove **blame** from, disregarding as trivial, or granting exemption. The project management definition of excuses is passing blame for one's **failure** on to someone or something else, or defending one's incompetence by claiming **helplessness**.

The Sin

Proactive risk management increases the success of our projects. Excuses, however, limit our ability to successfully mitigate risks since they conceal reality and obscure potential problems that might negatively affect the project. Projects are riddled with excuses; not a single project gets executed without them. All stakeholders, including the project manager, use excuses on projects. Most are innocent: "I'm sorry I'm late, I was stuck in traffic" (actually, I left my house too late), "I have been having email problems, could you resend that request?" (actually, I saw your email but have not yet taken the time to respond), or "the vendor is late in delivering" (because I provided the requirements late).

Many believe that it is human nature to make excuses; more likely, it is our bad habits that make us find excuses for what went wrong or what we were not able to do. We tend to be over-optimistic about our own abilities and often bite off more than we can chew. To deal with the situation this creates, we search for explanations (read: excuses) for our own failures, so we do not lose face.

Why bother correcting this bad habit? Jeffrey Pfeffer, in a *Business 2.0* article (May 2005), said it best:

> As the saying goes, the definition of insanity is doing the same thing over and over again and expecting the outcome to change. Excuses, therefore, drag organizations toward an insane, unprofitable end. As a (project) leader, it's your job to counteract them. Or don't, and you and your team can trade excuses all day about why you're unemployed.

A Case of Excuses

This headline in *Wired* magazine shows how excuses can negatively affect not just a specific project but an entire American industry: "Detroit Rarely Misses a Chance to Miss a Chance" (Ben Mack, December 5, 2008). A classic example in the automotive industry is hybrid cars. While the Big Three automakers in Detroit were making numerous excuses not to invest in their hybrid projects ("hybrids are too expensive to build," "people will not buy them"), the market changed significantly. Now, Japanese car manufacturers can barely keep up with demand and Detroit might not survive long enough to catch up.

Excuses can be most destructive and costly toward the end of a project or even after the project has failed. Although it was perhaps triggered by the current economic downturn, the Big

Three crisis has long been in the making. Bad business decisions (for example, to finance current high-margin projects like SUVs and trucks) were followed by excuses not to finance projects that were bound to be needed when economic times changed.

Danger Signs

Many of us have the habit of making excuses in all different environments: at home, at work, to family and friends. We are so good at it that it we sometimes don't even realize we are doing it. The good news is, like any bad habit, we can change it! Experts agree that we can change a behavior; the catch is that it takes a minimum of 21 days to do so. As with any bad habit, change starts with admitting we have a problem.

Solutions

To come to grips with excuses in any workplace, follow this 12-step program. This set of guiding principles outlines a course for recovering from this bad behavior:

1. Admit that you have been **powerless** over excuses and that your projects have become unmanageable.

2. Realize that people around you use excuses because it is hard to acknowledge that they have done a poor job.

3. Make a list of all persons you have harmed with excuses, and make amends with them (except when doing so would injure them or others).

4. Do not give up before you have started. Genuinely seek to create an excuse-free project environment. For others to follow you, you need to believe in it yourself.

5. Decide to change your course of actions and become the project role model for admitting your mistakes instead of making excuses.

6. Treat this like a project: Develop a plan for achieving the goal and set a deadline for its attainment.

7. Find a project sponsor for your "banishing excuses" project and involve executive management so they can inspire people and lead by example.

8. Implement a project excuses jar as a vehicle for creating an excuse-free project environment. (see Tips below.)

9. Recognize excuses when they happen and address them on the spot.

10. Celebrate small wins. When people see the payoff of avoiding excuses they will be more inclined to join you in your effort and change their habits.

11. Stick with it! Change is never easy, especially when it involves changing habits that protect you.

12. Carry the no-excuses message to all the people you work with, and practice these principles in all your projects.

The key, of course, is not to get discouraged and give up after slipping back into the bad behavior of using excuses. Analyze what went wrong and why, plan to overcome the obstacles, and try, try again!

Tips for Eliminating Excuses

▶ During your project kickoff meeting, spend some time on the issue of excuses, their negative impact on the project, and how to break this bad habit.

▶ With your project team, *look at the calendar, count ahead 21 days, and mark the date as when the project is excuse-free!*

▶ *Create a project excuses jar;* whenever someone uses an excuse, she has to deposit $5 in the jar. This way everyone is involved in making sure there are no excuses and the jar revenue can be used for a team fun event. Changing behavior always works better if (1) it is a fun experience and (2) there are awards and penalties involved.

30

Failure

Failure is an act or instance of proving unsuccessful; lack of success. In project management, failure may mean different things to different stakeholders.

The Sin

What does failure mean in project management? Do we mean failure to deliver the project's outcomes/deliverables/objectives/scope on time, within budget, and to the specified quality? Or do we mean failure to deliver the benefits as outlined in the project's business case (project charter)? An IT system may be delivered on time by an IT contractor but prove useless to the customer. Is this a failed project? Likewise, a construction contractor may fail to make any profit on a development that is late but the client may still benefit significantly from its delivery. Is this a failed project?

In many approaches to project management, the project manager is judged on the delivery of outcomes whereas the sponsor is judged on the delivery of benefits. It is therefore possible that a project can be a failure for the project manager yet a success for the sponsor and vice versa.

Failure in projects, particularly IT projects, is common, as detailed in various reports by research firms like the Standish Group and Gartner. However, most projects fail to deliver outcomes on time, within budget, and to specification or fail to deliver the predicted benefits because in hindsight it was never possible to achieve either of these results; in other words, we set out to fail. Perhaps our true failure lies in not appreciating the inherent uncertainties and therefore performing inadequate risk management. Without formal risk management or sensitivity analysis, we have no idea of the true likelihood of the project's achieving its **promises**. We therefore over-promise and under-deliver.

As project managers, we always seem to underestimate how long it will take and how much it will cost to implement a project, and to overestimate the benefits the project will deliver. Perhaps this bias toward optimism is just human nature; it certainly seems to be prevalent throughout project management. Once a project gets the go-ahead and is underway, it is very difficult to stop.

We have all heard that it is "better to seek forgiveness than ask for permission." In project management, we often set targets that we know we can't achieve, rather than be realistic. When we are late or over budget, we say we are sorry but of course it is then too late.

Several Cases of Failure

Three projects that illustrate failure are the London Millennium Dome, the London Eye, and Shell's Bonga oil field development. The first two projects were part of the UK's millennium celebrations.

The dome situated on the Greenwich Meridian in London was completed on time and to specification, but over budget—you could say that two out of three for a time-constrained project isn't bad. The dome was to be a visitor attraction to celebrate the new millennium but unfortunately the visitors didn't come. As a result, the benefits anticipated in the business case never materialized and the project was considered a failure. In hindsight, it seems the initial business case was based on the number of visitors needed to make the project economically feasible rather than any real market research.

The London Eye, a ferris wheel situated a few miles up river from the dome, had problems in its commissioning phase and opened three months late. Today it is one of London's premier tourist attractions—30 million people had ridden on it by June 2008—and it is a big business success. Its lease has been extended, and it will become a key feature of London's Olympic Games in 2012.

Shell's project to deliver offshore production facilities in the Bonga oil field was fraught with problems largely attributable to poor risk management, which led to inaccurate estimates and unrealistic plans. Completed more than two years late and approximately $2 billion over budget, it is now one of the world's largest producing oil fields. All the early failures seem to have been forgotten.

Danger Signs

One easy way to determine if a project is likely to fail is to ask: "What is the chance of achieving that?" Or, when talking about time and cost: "What is the earliest date we could complete and the minimum cost?" or "What is the latest we might complete and the maximum cost?"

Few project managers will be able to answer these questions. They are not even aware they are planning to fail and are therefore proceeding with blind optimism. An encouraging answer would be along the lines of: "We have 40 percent confidence of achieving the planned end date, but we could be one month earlier if things progress well; we could be two months late if we are unlucky."

The textbooks tell us that the answer must be in the execution or implementation phase of the project, where the cost of fixing an error or changing something is most extreme. However, failure is most destructive after the project outcomes have been delivered and when users/stakeholders refuse to accept the end product because it fails to meet their requirements. At this point, unless remedial action is taken promptly, the project will never recover. The Millennium Dome in London is an example of this.

Solutions

The philosopher Niccolò Machiavelli noted that small problems are hard to detect yet easy to fix. But let them develop and they will become easy to detect but hard to fix.

Project failure can be prevented in the early phases of the lifecycle by sufficient, appropriate planning. The outcome of the planning process should be a project management plan that takes into account the true context of the project, its novelty, uniqueness, **politics**, etc. What the users/stakeholders really need and expect, their acceptance criteria and tolerances, and all the uncertainties and risks involved (with an allowance for the "unknown unknowns") should be considered. Only by developing a plan in this way can the project manager minimize the project's chance of failure.

Tips for Avoiding Failure

▶ *Think carefully about how you define project success.* Delivering a project on time, within budget, and to specification does not necessarily mean that it will be a business success. Likewise, a project that is late, over budget, and perhaps lacking in quality (see **shoddy quality**) can still be a business success.

▶ *Pay attention to lessons learned.* Projects that fail for whatever reason and where the project manager and team do not learn any lessons can be considered a double failure. Conversely, perhaps a failed project that prevents other future projects from failing should not be considered a total failure.

31

Favoritism

Favoritism is defined as the act of favoring one person or group over others with equal claims; partiality. In project management, showing favoritism is assigning project responsibilities based on relationships rather than skills.

The Sin

A project manager or team member is often assigned to work on a project based on subjective factors. People naturally want to be comfortable with those around them, so they sometimes give people they know positions despite a lack of qualifications. If the project team members see another team member being favored in hiring or in work assignments, it will create **conflict** within the team. This conflict may in turn affect many aspects of the project.

All team members want to be treated fairly. They expect a uniform set of rules for everyone on the team. Changing the rules for one team member can cause others to shut down, affect production and capacity, and stifle creativity. In the worst cases, team members may start to rebel; they will lose respect (see **disrespect**) for the person playing favorites as well as for the person being favored.

A Case of Favoritism

A project director had the opportunity to hire some project managers. The director hired people he had worked with in the past, even though they had limited project management skills. The inexperienced project managers were unable to manage the project effectively, resulting in an unsuccessful project.

Team members quickly became frustrated as they tried to fill in the gaps where the project managers fell short. Of course, not all team members were qualified to complete project management duties in addition to their own functions, so delays in the project resulted.

As others felt they had to pitch in to do the work of the project director's "favorites" to complete project deliverables, the team's morale plummeted.

Danger Signs

Sometimes it is easy to tell if favoritism was a factor in hiring a new project manager or team member. Do the person's background, education, and expertise match the requirements to get the job done? Have the hiring manager and the new hire worked together in the past?

Favoritism is in the hands of the person doing the hiring. To avoid favoritism, the project manager should clearly define the project responsibilities and make sure the candidate meets those requirements. The project manager should act fairly by treating all team members based on the requirements of their project roles.

If a team feels that favoritism has influenced hiring decisions, it will be difficult to get people to work with someone they don't respect. Key information may not be given to the "favorite," which will continue to cause problems later in the project.

Tips for Eliminating Favoritism

▶ *Identify job requirements and hire based on skills.*

▶ *Communicate the skills of the new person with the entire team.*

▶ *Treat project team members in accordance with the requirements of their project roles.*

▶ *Clearly define project roles and responsibilities.*

▶ *Assign work based on objective factors.*

▶ *Be sensitive to the needs of the team.*

32

Fragmentation

Fragmentation is the act or process of disintegrating so as to create incomplete or isolated parts or portions (see **isolation**); the state of breaking off into detached parts. In project management, fragmentation is easily recognized in teams that are unable to perform as a cohesive, unified group.

The Sin

Some of the best projects are delivered by teams of individuals who are able to work together synergistically. In this environment, team members effectively leverage each other's talents, support each other, and do whatever is required to meet a unified objective. Creating such an environment, however, can be a daunting task.

Project managers must first recognize that projects usually operate within the context of matrix management, with team members pulled from many different organizational units. Without exception, each member of the team will describe his or her respective organizational unit as "the place where I work" or "the group I'm in." It's also the place that provides their paycheck. It's natural for them to feel loyalty toward this unit.

In contrast, projects and project teams nearly always cut across organizational boundaries. Projects typically seek to create an outcome or change that is intended to benefit the entire organization. Inevitably, this will require give-and-take within the project team. Therein lies the rub: The best interests, inclinations, and preferred courses of action of any given project may be in direct conflict with those of a participating individual's organizational unit. This is where fragmentation of the team can make an entrance.

People who join project teams often bring baggage on board. This baggage comes in the form of personal and professional objectives that are directly tied to their "home base." They believe that they were hired to fulfill a particular mission, often related to their organizational unit. Technology people want to advance technology. Marketing people are conditioned to do whatever is needed to sell things. Operational folks aim to run an effective, revenue-generating operation.

If left unchecked, these differing objectives can break the team away from being a single-minded entity and into separate parts or portions. Individual team members will become detached parts—the very definition of fragmentation.

A Case of Fragmentation

One of the worst cases of fragmentation I've ever seen came on a project conducted at a large company. The mission was to design and install an automated system in one of the company's major manufacturing divisions.

The engineering team felt strongly about the need to push the state-of-the-art technology for this manufacturing system (after all, that's what technology people do). Unfortunately, the reality was that this system was to be installed in a production area staffed with non-technical individuals. For a variety of reasons, this is what the production rep on the team (the client) wanted.

The engineering team considered its overarching mission to be to "continually advance the state-of-the-art by implementing leading edge technologies." On this particular project, however, doing so would require the installation of a system that was considerably more complex than needed. Moreover, operating such a system was well beyond the capabilities of the client division's operational and maintenance staff. Each side had its own perspective—and lobbied vigorously. The engineers argued that the company would fail to move forward without a push for higher levels of technology. The manufacturing division argued that, to make money, they needed simple solutions and cost-effective staffing plans.

The result was fragmentation. As each side clung to its position, they stopped communicating for an extended period of time. By the time they reconnected, it was too late. The engineers had developed a solution that was unacceptable to the customer. Much time and money had been wasted. The team literally disintegrated; they disbanded and a new team was formed.

Danger Signs

When the glue that binds a team together begins to disintegrate, it's likely that fragmentation is not far behind. As project manager or team lead, you must keep a sharp eye out for this disintegration. Be sensitive to reduced levels of cooperation across the team.

Look for elevated levels of quibbling and infighting. Notice when team members seem to be drawing territorial lines—typically across organizational boundaries. In short, be aware of a lack of give-and-take when it comes to project issues, as well as a general lack of spirit to rally behind a common cause. All these danger signs are manifestations of **conflict** that will lead to fragmentation if they are not resolved quickly and effectively.

Solutions

Many project managers find conflict resolution either distasteful or incredibly difficult. Addressing and resolving conflict requires a certain amount of strength on the part of the project manager. In the case above, the project manager's style was extremely conciliatory. She avoided conflict at all costs. She spent all her time and energy on relationship management, trying to get the team members to get along.

In fact, the relationship problems did not arise until well into the project and were a direct result of conflict related to differing objectives. Recognizing differing objectives within the team requires a savvy project manager, one who is able to appreciate that not every team member will automatically line up behind the singular vision for the project.

Tips for Preventing Fragmentation

▶ *Start from the start.* From day 1, assertively establish that partisan **politics** is unacceptable. Urge the team to always be thinking of what is best for the project.

▶ *Acknowledge, acknowledge, acknowledge.* Hit the issue head-on; openly acknowledge that team member are not always going to get along perfectly. Urge the team to seek resolution through confrontation (in the classic conflict resolution sense) before allowing rifts to form between team members.

▶ *Remain ever-vigilant.* Don't just request and record data at team meetings. Carefully watch body language and communication patterns. Look out for any behaviors or conduct that suggests an interpersonal storm may be brewing.

33

Gaming

Gaming is defined as playing games of chance for stakes; risking something of value on the outcome of something involving chance. In project management, gaming the system means using the rules, policies, and procedures of a system to achieve what gets counted instead of what really counts.

The Sin

When a project manager puts too many rules in place, makes them vague, or is unaware of the consequences of those rules, project team members—who study the rules closely—can use this massive (often contradictory) rule set to play the "game" their own, often unexpected way. Overly optimistic project deadlines, creative counting, fear of taking risks, and numerous unnecessary meetings are all symptoms of project team members gaming the system. Do your team members spend more time doing what gets measured at the expense of what really matters? Are they routinely responding to internal dynamics rather than external factors? Are they working toward organizational deadlines rather than the market environment? If so, the organization or project team has created the dynamic for gaming the system.

A Case of Gaming

During the 1960s Robert S. McNamara was the U.S. Secretary of Defense and an architect of the U.S. policy in Southeast Asia. Considered one of the "best and brightest" of the Kennedy administration, he had been hired by Ford Motor Company as one of ten former World War II officers known as the "whiz kids" who helped the company implement modern planning, organization, and management control systems. He advanced rapidly, eventually becoming the first person outside the Ford family to become president of the company.

During President Kennedy's time in office and continuing into the early part of President Johnson's term, the American commitment in South Vietnam steadily increased. In 1965, in response to stepped-up military activity by the nationalist Viet Cong in South Vietnam and their North Vietnamese allies, the United States began bombing North Vietnam, deployed large military forces, and entered into combat in South Vietnam. McNamara's plan, supported by requests from top U.S. military commanders in Vietnam, led to the commitment of almost 535,000 troops by June 1968.

As the number of troops and the intensity of fighting escalated, McNamara put in place a statistical strategy for victory in Vietnam. He concluded that there were a limited number of Viet Cong fighters in Vietnam and that a war of attrition would destroy them: "The body count was a measurement of the adversary's manpower losses; we undertook it because one of Westy's [General Westmoreland's] objectives was to reach a so-called crossover point, at which Viet Cong and North Vietnamese casualties would be greater than they could sustain." Unfortunately, this technocratic, problem-solving modus operandi turned out to be ill-suited to the vagaries of jungle warfare in Vietnam.

McNamara's macabre accounting protocol fell victim to the most basic flaw of systems analysis: garbage in, garbage out. "Ah les statistiques," a South Vietnamese officer once said of McNamara, "your Secretary of Defense loves statistics. We Vietnamese can give him all he wants. If you want them to go up, they will go up. If you want them to go down, they will go down." As McNamara himself admitted, the data reported back from the battlefront as often as not were erroneous, and Washington heard only what it wanted to hear.

In this case the costs were catastrophic: The American public had been led to believe the war was being won only to find out in 1968 that this simply was not the truth. The costs to the country in terms of men, materiel, and morale continued to be felt for decades.

Danger Signs

The project manager and team members all need to understand the dynamics at play in an organization or project team that creates the ability to game the system as well as ways to mitigate effects. The warning signs that gaming is going on include overly long meetings that lack productivity, a scarcity of innovation, and a preoccupation with the means rather than the end.

Solutions

The project manager must be able to recognize that achieving various metrics does not equate to accomplishing the final result. The two should go hand in hand, but when project team members find out that what gets measured is what matters, the system has become corrupted and must be changed.

Tips for Addressing Gaming

▶ *Be able to recognize behaviors that are detrimental* to long-term success.

▶ *Define clear-cut outcomes* so you can recognize when they are achieved.

▶ *Ensure that project team members are doing what needs to be done* and not focusing exclusively on what gets measured.

34

Guessing

Guessing is forming an opinion from little or no evidence, or reaching a conclusion through conjecture, chance, or intuition. We all know that a project is a finite undertaking to attain a unique objective. Since a project has no unequivocal predecessor, we must estimate almost all its attributes. This can be done with a variety of techniques, but guessing (generally called estimating in project management) becomes a sin when we don't expend the appropriate energy to gather sufficient information or properly use the techniques. Too often, we are guessing not only about a project plan, but even about which projects to initiate.

The Sin

Guessing is the bane of project managers, but very common and often necessary. By their nature, projects require estimates of scope and the required tasks, durations, costs, resources, and associated risks. Planning estimates based on incomplete knowledge or effort (guesses) generally produce cost overruns, late or incomplete projects, and a poor-quality result (see **shoddy qual-**

ity). "Accurate time estimates" is on the wish list of every project management office. To be safe, however, staff resources almost always include extra time in their task duration estimates. The estimates have three components: (1) "hands-on" time—the time the work probably could be completed if there were no interruptions, (2) additional time required because of multitasking that entails unproductive "set down" and "set up" time, and (3) safety time to ensure on-time task delivery in case an unforeseen problem arises. It would appear that projects should always finish early, but because of human behavioral issues, this extra task time (and more) is usually expended. Even if a task is completed early, most staff members hesitate to admit it and endanger their credibility on the next guess.

Another problem occurs when stakeholders outside the project implementation do the guessing. Owners of the project, for example, may believe that the project is performing as expected if they have no information to the contrary. Lack of communication can have significant consequences for project funding if the project burn rate is higher than expected. Negative surprises frequently result in loss of confidence in the project team. Sometimes even the project team members lack knowledge of changes or unresolved issues. This will definitely cause problems when project integration is attempted. The project manager must maintain open, timely, and accurate communications channels with all stakeholders.

A Case of Guessing

When my IT service company acquired a similar, but failing company, the plan was to convert what was left of their dwindling client base to our existing system. What I soon discovered was that clients were leaving because, although many great technical projects were underway, the users hadn't been getting the features they needed.

The staff had been guessing that the wonderful technical features they kept adding to the system would impress their clients. They didn't—they just made the entire system more complex. At first, the clients asked, then complained, and finally just began leaving. The company had no formal process for discovering what clients really wanted; the IT staff expended much of their energy running projects they thought were interesting but that were the wrong projects for the customers.

We held some very active client meetings and while we were too late for some users, for the most part we were able to turn the situation around. We kept the site operating and eventually added new clients.

Guessing about which projects to work on is even more deadly then guessing about task times on a project plan. Nothing is more frustrating or expensive than discovering halfway through a serious project commitment that work is being done on the wrong problem or improvement.

If the organization does not have a corporate plan and policy for setting priorities, resource managers, project managers, or even project salespeople will set the priorities. Not setting priorities, or not correcting guesses as more information becomes available, causes many additional project sins.

It's difficult to tell just how much a failed process costs a company. The ramifications for owners, employees, and the community are enormous. In this case, many of the employees had been promised a share in the company's success, but, of course, that never happened. It was difficult to retain some of the staff even when we decided to keep the operation. Like many of my staff, my personal costs were some very, very long hours and the accompanying family disruptions.

Even when just one project is negatively impacted by guessing, the results can be devastating. As a project overruns its planned cost and schedule, management can forget the original objective and inject additional problems or the project team itself can modify its efforts in negative ways. The final deliverable of a project built on uncorrected guesses seldom accomplishes its full intended value. The project team loses confidence in both itself and the organization. An organization's entire project management program can lose value and start a downward cycle.

Danger Signs

In the acquisition example presented above, the danger signs were everywhere: Clients complained and the company was losing business. In the early days of computers, the technology was a black box to most of the world except for the technical insiders. I'm afraid the technicians wanted to keep it that way and exploit the collateral power. More than once, I have seen this power-hoarding attitude shut out good business processes. In the company we acquired, the clients were ignored in favor of what technicians believed (guessed) they wanted.

For the more general problem of guessing about the project plan, project managers can use tools such as earned value (EV) reports to provide early warning signs. Earned value also has an emerging practice involving the use of margins (a time task with no work scope inserted on project baselines) that can be used to absorb known risk such as that involving the completion of multiple paths prior to joining a critical path. Consumption of one of these margin tasks can help predict project completion status. EV margins are somewhat like the safety buffers of critical chain project management, which promotes buffers at path intersections and at the end of the project to handle project uncertainties. With critical chain, a "traffic light" indicator of buffer penetration provides advance warning of possible problems.

Solutions

An organization must have a process for addressing the views of contrarians to avoid group think (see **consensus**), which can cause an organization to proceed too far down the wrong road. Sometimes unpopular opinions still have very good points that must be addressed to avoid future pain (see **popularity**).

In a more general sense, we must learn to use available project management tools more wisely and learn from past mistakes— the lessons learned of project management.

The lifeline for project planning is that several estimating tools and methods address uncertainty. Some of the more common techniques are expert opinion, specific analogy, bottom-up, parametric, limitation by availability of resources, algorithmic modeling, case-based reasoning, and COCOMO (COnstructive COst MOdel) for software projects. A very progressive tool is the use of artificial neural networks. The good-old-fashioned-way is trend analysis: Make an initial estimate using one or more of these techniques and adjust the plan as the project progresses and more information becomes available.

Tips for Eliminating Guessing

▶ *Always establish appropriate expectations.* Even when the best estimates are made, they are still estimates.

▶ *Provide date ranges or express varying confidence levels in possible date ranges.* Whenever possible, describe estimates in association with the required resources.

▶ *Control or at least account for the fact that guessing sometimes leads to uncontrolled scope* **creep**. Whatever else the project manager does, realizing this is critical.

▶ *Switch emphasis from on-time completion of tasks to on-time completion of projects.*

35

Haphazardness

Haphazardness is lack of order or planning; irregular; chance; random. In project management, haphazardness with regard to risk or uncertainty can doom a project from the start.

The Sin

All project managers understand that before undertaking a project they must engage in a planning process. This is necessary for any activities we intend to carry out, whether we think of them as projects or not. The problem is that in many projects, planning is done poorly, particularly with regard to accounting for *all* risks and uncertainties that have the potential to affect a project. This inadequate planning can lead to random responses to problems that arise on the project. Failing to plan thoroughly for risk and uncertainties, including developing risk responses, creates haphazardness on the project. In effect, haphazardness is both a cause and an effect in projects because haphazard planning causes the haphazard execution of projects.

Unfortunately, haphazardness is quite common in project management. While most project managers make some effort to manage risks, the analysis and subsequent planning they undertake are often inadequate. For example, most project managers perform qualitative risk analysis in that they identify, prioritize, and work to mitigate risks. However, most project managers fail to perform quantitative risk analysis and therefore have no data about the actual impacts (in cost or duration) these risks can have on their project.

Inadequate risk analysis and management manifest themselves in missed budgets, missed deadlines, poor quality, or failed projects.

A Case of Haphazardness

Oil companies operate in a highly volatile environment. Oil prices may change dramatically, costs and resources fluctuate in completely different cycles, and highly expensive exploration activities may turn out to be uneconomic. Furthermore, energy projects can be measured in decades while prices, costs, and regulations can change over much shorter timeframes. Those organizations that are the quickest to adapt to changing circumstances usually perform better. Realtors commonly attribute success in their business to "location, location, location." Oil executives might see their success as based on "cycles, cycles, cycles."

At the end of the 1990s, oil prices dropped dramatically. In reaction, many oil companies began to curtail the number of their active projects. Some were able to react to the changing circumstances quickly based on their prior planning. Understanding that their business was especially prone to large swings in the business cycle, they preserved cash and planned their projects accordingly; they had accounted for this possibility in their projects' inception phase. Other companies attempted to run their exploration and production operations for as long as possible. When they started to experience cash flow problems, they suspended most of their projects and laid off much of their workforce. When oil prices rebounded, exploration and production activities restarted apace. Those companies that had planned with the business cycle in mind were able to quickly restart operations and were able to hire the best of the available talent from the laid-off workforce. Others did not fare as well.

Danger Signs

Early signs of haphazardness in a project manifest themselves in the planning and analysis regarding potential risks and uncertainty. Inadequate planning can often be seen in the evolution of risk identification and analysis. For example, the initial version of the risk management document may identify four major schedule risks. Do later versions identify additional risks? Have potential impacts changed as risks have become better understood and mitigation activities have been undertaken? A static or nearly static risk document often indicates that insufficient care and attention have been directed to this area.

Haphazardness is an equal opportunity sin, as its cost to projects can accrue at any time. However, it is most destructive when its effects are masked until late in a project. Once haphazardness becomes evident, it can be mitigated to a certain extent. But the longer the project has run before the effects become apparent, the greater the costs that will be incurred in the form of changes in scope or project **failure**.

Solutions

Projects fail or succeed based on how well risk and uncertainty are understood and managed. Whether it is uncertainty in material costs or political risk, all risks and uncertainties must be thoroughly understood and incorporated into the project plan. Haphazard planning will result in haphazard execution.

Tips for Overcoming Haphazardness

▶ As part of project planning, *identify all previous similar projects or activities* that have taken place in the organization and review risk management activities, including risk lists, mitigation plans, response plans, and the success of prior risk management efforts.

▶ *Maintain a historical record* of previous project outcomes, including risks. A list of risks, associated activities, and outcomes can be as simple as a table or as involved as a risk register.

▶ *Review project performance* regularly.

▶ *Adapt project plans* based on the results of your review.

36
Helplessness

Helplessness is being unable to help oneself; being weak or dependent; deprived of strength or power; powerless; incapacitated. In project management, helplessness is the belief or perception that a project manager does not have the strength, knowledge, or power necessary to lead the project to a successful conclusion. This perception may be true or false, but it is always debilitating.

The Sin

Project managers are all a little bit like Blanche DuBois, the lead character in *A Streetcar Named Desire*: We "rely on the kindness of strangers." A certain degree of helplessness is inevitable; project managers almost never have sufficient formal power to meet the challenges of a given project. We often do not directly supervise key project team members; we do not choose our assigned level of resources; and we report to customers and managers who aren't technically part of the project team but whose actions are crucial to a project's success.

Project managers who rely too heavily on formal or official power to lead their projects are particularly susceptible to helplessness. Symptoms include project paralysis (while the hapless project manager seeks salvation from higher management), **confusion**, panic, and substandard performance.

A Case of Helplessness

In the *Challenger* disaster, perceived helplessness on the part of managers, engineers, and executives combined to create an atmosphere in which essential technical input was rejected in the face of perceived irresistible political and media pressure. Engineers from Thiokol protested that the O-rings might fail if the temperature dropped below freezing. NASA leadership, concerned about public criticism if the launch kept being delayed, dismissed those technical concerns. The result was an ill-judged launch.

Many critics and analysts fault NASA management, but the engineers involved had responsibilities as well. When people don't listen to your argument, it's obvious the argument isn't getting through. Repeating the same argument is like talking really slowly to someone who doesn't speak your language and hoping your message gets across. It's time to change your approach.

The Thiokol engineers kept insisting that their technical judgment be accepted and did not try to help managers solve their very real concern. After a while, the managers moved on, shutting the engineers out of the final decision.

The engineers felt helpless in the face of management pressure, but they weren't. If one argument fails, it's time to try a different approach. Perceived helplessness on the part of the engineers cut them out of the process and ensured they would fail to influence the final decision. Seven people died and the shuttle program was dealt a blow from which it has never completely recovered.

Danger Signs

Perceived helplessness is a common project risk, ready to strike anytime and anywhere. Assume your project will be affected unless you take the necessary steps to overcome it.

Tips for Eliminating Helplessness

▶ *Realize that you're never completely helpless—or all-powerful.* Everyone has strengths; everyone has limitations.

▶ *Maximize your informal power.* Roles and resources are given to you by others, on loan. However, the respect you earn, the rhetoric you command, and the relationships you develop build your power in ways you own and you control.

▶ *Think creatively.* It may be the case that a given road or direction is blocked and there's no way around. However, there's often another road you can take.

37

Hope

Hope is the belief or expectation that something wished for can or will happen. In a well-planned-out project, hope is not required. If hope outweighs clear tasks and outcomes, the project manager would be wise to focus more on planning for the project.

The Sin

Of all the project management sins, hope may be the worst. Hope means you are counting on something good happening or something bad not happening—which means you're not in control of what actually does happen. Hope simply cannot compensate for **poor planning** or a lack of control.

All project managers are familiar with scope **creep**, that insidious slow growth in the product requirements. But how many are familiar with hope creep? Hope creep is lying on a status report (see **prevarication**), hoping you can make up the deficit before the next status report. Not a good thing, but too common.

Because every stage of a project builds on what was done earlier in the project, placing your faith in hope is most dangerous at the beginning. Toward the end of the project, you can hope that the new software will pass testing without serious bugs; if it doesn't, the schedule and cost impact will be relatively minor. But if you're hoping that the project "goes well" even though you didn't spend any time gathering requirements or planning, then the project will almost certainly face serious issues down the road.

The greatest danger in relying on hope instead of planning and preparation is that doing so will inhibit the project manager from effectively dealing with problems as they arise. In project management many decisions have both a short-term and a long-term impact. If the project is not well planned, fixing a problem in the short term may cause more significant problems in the long term. Without a plan, the "law of unintended consequences" is certain to kick in and create serious issues for the project in the future.

A Case of Misguided Hope

In a project management class several years ago, two of my students were marine engineers. They were under commission to design and build a 100-foot yacht for a local factory owner. The owner had not given them a budget, but had told them he wanted the yacht completed within three years.

After two years the owner asked the engineers how much longer the yacht was going to take. They said they had no idea. He then asked them how much more money it was going to cost beyond the $2 million they had already spent. Again, they said they had no idea.

The factory owner told the engineers that if they didn't take a project management class he was going to fire them and hire someone who knew what they were doing. They ended up in my class.

When we were discussing planning in the class, the two engineers admitted they had just started designing the yacht and hadn't planned anything out except the design—no work breakdown structure, no schedule, no budget, no risk analysis. They had just hoped that everything would work out. Of course, the engineers' naïve hope that the yacht would be finished in three years almost cost them their jobs.

Danger Signs

Unfortunately, it is difficult to recognize when too much faith is being placed in hope. After all, even experienced project managers sometimes find themselves hoping that everything will go as planned—or worse, will "go well." But when you find yourself hoping that the project will go well instead of knowing that it will, consider that a red flag that you haven't prepared well enough.

Solutions

The project manager should try to anticipate and prepare for every possible outcome. When the project is well planned and the project manager is in control, there is no need to "hope" that something will happen. Of course, the project manager cannot control all aspects of a project, such as external influences. The project manager should specifically include those aspects in the risk plan and develop plans to deal with them if they occur.

Most of all, don't depend on hope to keep your project afloat. As the management guru Peter Drucker once said: "You can either take action, or you can sit back and wait for a miracle. Miracles are great, but they are so unpredictable."

Tips for Keeping Hope from Misleading Your Project

▶ *Review your project management plan.*

▶ *Validate and revalidate your requirements* as you go through the project.

▶ *Perform a risk analysis* and keep it updated.

38

Immaturity

Immaturity usually applies to a person or object that has not reached complete growth or is not yet ready to perform a particular function. In project management, the term is often used to describe an inadequacy in a commonly recognized discipline, such as planning or organizing.

The Sin

In describing a person as immature, we consider not only physical immaturity, but also emotional, social, educational, financial, and behavioral immaturity. In project management, immaturity generally connotes an inadequate capability in one or more of the commonly recognized disciplines of management: planning, organizing, staffing, and controlling. Often, a fifth discipline, learning, is included. Several views of project management characterize them differently, but these disciplines make up its common base.

Immaturity has three distinct possible sources. The first and most obvious is the project manager or project management team.

The second is a lack of capability in one or more of the organization's processes or procedures. The third is immaturity in any of the other groups or functions that form the organizational context in which the project operates.

When considering level of maturity, we should expect the 80/20 rule to be true. That is, about 20 percent of the organizations executing projects are operating at a relatively high level of maturity in all aspects of project management, including their project management teams, processes, and procedures. That means that about 80 percent of organizations are immature in at least one aspect of project management, and certainly some organizations are immature across the board. How that immaturity manifests itself is still somewhat probabilistic and indirect. The less mature, the more likely there are related problems in the execution and results of projects. The less mature, the less able the organization is to recognize the cause of those problems.

Immaturity certainly increases the probability that a project will fail in some respect, but many projects will succeed despite immaturity. Sometimes immaturity will result in lost opportunity, such as the project's being late or costing more than it should have; then, too, it might finish sooner and cost less because certain things that should have been done were not. Sometimes immaturity will manifest itself as a problem of **shoddy quality** in the project deliverable.

Mature organizations have projects that fail and grossly immature organizations have projects that succeed. The difference is the probability of these events occurring. There is also the ambiguity of how we measure project success. A product that is never used will never show any quality problems. A canceled project will never know how close it came to being a black hole for resources. It is very rare that a project fails in some aspect because someone wanted it to; more often the **failure** is attributable to a lack of maturity in those areas needed to make it succeed. Perhaps the right things were known and just not done, needs were not recognized, or the project team or management was not capable of taking the right actions.

Danger Signs

Looking at the five disciplines, lack of maturity in planning will result in **chaos** and lots of unplanned activity and abandoned plans. Failures in planning, which include inadequately communicating with customers and sponsors and identifying requirements completely, are the most destructive and costly mistakes a project can make.

Immaturity in organizing is commonly seen in under- or over-staffing and a mismatch of skills and capabilities to the assigned tasks. Staffing immaturity displays symptoms similar to immaturity in organizing, including frequent mismatches between the types and numbers of people needed to accomplish tasks.

Controlling immaturity often manifests itself as general **confusion** about what was to be done, when tasks were to be done, and the status and progress of the project.

Probably the worst impact for immaturity on a project relates to the discipline of learning. Immaturity in learning dooms subsequent projects to repeat the same problems.

Solutions

The greatest lesson in addressing project performance and improvement by looking at maturing project management capability is that it is a true moving target. Weakness in one area will consistently manifest itself as a problem, no matter what you do in any of the other areas. Improvement in one area will not improve your results until you have resolved the mismatch in the other areas.

The best solution is to develop a comprehensive definition of maturity that addresses all the management disciplines and sets forth ways to measure and to improve.

Tips for Overcoming Immaturity

▶ *Define and assess the maturity of the team and the organization* in each of the five project management disciplines: planning, organizing, staffing, controlling, and learning.

▶ *Clearly define measurements for success* for all aspects of the project.

▶ *Communicate the definitions of success* to all stakeholders.

39

Inattentiveness

Inattentiveness is a failure to focus or concentrate on the matter at hand. In project management, inattentiveness means not paying enough attention to the significant tasks, issues, risks, or stakeholders in a project. Project managers sometimes wrongly focus on the easy things, simply because they are easy and can lead to a sense of accomplishment.

The Sin

Inattentiveness can be a common project management sin, especially with new project managers or those who, by their nature, avoid **conflict**. It is also more common these days, as we try to do more with less and project managers are responsible for managing multiple teams and multiple projects. Project team members can also suffer from inattentiveness to their project because they are distracted with responsibilities for their "day jobs" or operational duties.

Inattentiveness takes a toll on a project when:

▸ The project manager focuses on noncritical tasks instead of critical ones

---

- A project manager responsible for many projects does not give equal attention to all

- Team members cannot focus on project tasks because they are dealing with production issues

- The project manager does not see—or ignores—unhappy team members or other project stakeholders and therefore cannot address their issues adequately.

Inattentiveness is most likely to occur during project planning and project execution. If certain aspects of the project are not planned for, they will be missing in execution. If you take the time to plan for the critical elements of the project, it will be easier to focus and pay attention to them. Inattentiveness is often the result of surprises caused by issues that were not worked out during the planning phase.

Execution, when the rubber meets the road, is also an easy phase for inattentiveness to set in, due to the sheer amount of work going on. Prioritization will help the project manager focus on the right things first.

A Case of Inattentiveness

A key stakeholder in my project was very negative and difficult to work with. He began ignoring emails about the project and stopped attending meetings. Instead of paying more attention to him, I became inattentive because it was the easy thing to do at the time. When it came to the final signoff of the project, he would not approve the deliverables because his complaints had not been addressed. My inattentiveness just delayed the inevitable issues to a point where they became much more difficult to address. This was a tough lesson, but one that stuck!

The key cost of inattentiveness is project success, however you measure it. If we fail to focus on the important elements of a project, we are much more at risk for delays, cost overruns, and unhappy customers.

Danger Signs

Warning signs of inattentiveness are critical tasks not completed on time, risks that are ignored, issues pending for a long period, and stakeholders or team members withdrawing from project communications.

Inattentiveness only delays project problems; it does not solve them. Make sure you see the warning signs and focus attention on potential pitfalls, however difficult or uncomfortable that may be.

Solutions

Prioritization and tracking are helpful tools. Both can be done with critical path scheduling for project tasks. Simply ranking and tracking issues and risks can help put the focus on critical items.

As for stakeholders and team members, making sure their voices are heard, looking for dissatisfaction, and addressing its ramifications are key. Prioritizing and tracking the organization's project portfolio can also help a project manager focus on the most important projects.

Tips for Battling Inattentiveness

▶ *Maintain open, constant communications* with all stakeholders.

▶ *Use prioritization methods* and critical path scheduling.

▶ *Surface and resolve issues* and risks as they arise.

▶ *Don't shy away from the difficult things;* they will hurt you in the end.

40

Indecision

Indecision is defined as the wavering between two or more courses of action or items. In project management, indecision can be on the part of an individual, who either cannot or chooses not to make a decision, or on the part of the project team, which fails to make a timely decision.

The Sin

Whether exhibited by an individual or a team, indecision delays the accomplishment of work. It is particularly detrimental when the work is on the critical path or involves critical resources. Unfortunately, the inability or unwillingness to make a decision is common in project management.

Sometimes people believe they don't have enough information and are therefore unwilling to make a decision. It is unusual for any person or group to have all the information they would like before making a decision. We rarely have 100 percent of the information we need. The successful project manager knows what information is most useful and seeks out that information as quickly as possible—and as early as possible in the project. The art of project management is knowing when you have just enough information to make a decision. Most project managers develop this ability through years of experience.

Sometimes people underestimate how difficult it will be to get a group to make a decision once they have the necessary information. This difficulty can be mitigated if a project team defines in advance which method will be used and who will make each type of decision. A charter, created at the beginning of the project, should answer these questions by specifying who makes which types of decisions.

Through the charter, the project manager should make certain that each member understands when and by whom decisions will be made. Empowerment is an overused term but it is relevant here. Empowerment doesn't mean dictating that "you make this decision"; rather, it means providing the tools to make the decision. This is especially important for those working at the lower levels. Project managers must ensure that their team members have the information they need to make decisions. Another tool is confidence. Instilling confidence in team members can help them overcome a natural hesitance to make decisions.

A Case of Indecision

When working with students, I've found that they often erroneously conclude that every group must come to a **consensus** before making a decision. A widespread misconception is that consensus is necessary for every group for every decision.

Reaching true consensus takes a great deal of time—and some decisions just aren't worth it. The indecision that results from trying unsuccessfully to get the group to agree can slow the project down and be detrimental to its eventual success.

In some cases, an individual with the right experience or knowledge will make a better decision than the group. I was part of a workshop in which we, as a group, had to work through problems and tests that involved survival training. We had to make a decision and we worked hard to reach consensus before deciding. One of the individuals in the group had actually gone through survival training and thus had firsthand experience. Unfortunately, we ignored the subject matter expert, favoring consensus, and got the decision wrong. We should have deferred to the subject matter expert on this decision.

Danger Signs

If no one acts as catalyst or leader on a project, indecision will result. Someone has to ask "when can we start?"

Procrastination is often a sign of indecision. Procrastination and indecision are closely connected.

Lack of a clear plan or charter showing who is able to make which types of decision can lead to the sin of indecision. Hesitancy in execution is also often caused by indecision.

A lack of confidence exhibited by either an individual or a team can lead to indecision. This is often the case for students or those who have less experience in project management.

Tips for Overcoming Indecision

▶ *Make a charter.* Be sure it specifies who will make which types of decision.

▸ *Create a communication plan.* This could be part of the charter or a separate document; like the charter, it will prove to be worth the time and effort.

▸ *Monitor the atmosphere in meetings and discussions.* Take time to create the proper environment so that team members feel empowered and free to make decisions.

41

Inefficiency

Inefficiency is defined as wasting time or effort in producing a result, or failing to produce the result. Unfortunately, the potential for inefficiency permeates every aspect of project management.

The Sin

The need for efficiency aligns with many of the constraints placed on the project manager. The competing demands of scope, time, cost, and quality—and arguably the other five knowledge areas of project management—often place absolute limits on what can be done. To maximize efficiency, the project manager must work to get the most utility possible out of any techniques and processes applied to the project. Although it is sometimes possible to go outside the constraints of the project to obtain additional resources, doing so can be difficult as well as damaging to the perception of the project and the team.

Inefficiency is rife in many projects. The fact that, by definition, a project must deliver a unique product, service, or result
means that every project faces new and different challenges. Any
waste of time poses a threat to another absolute in projects: their
temporary nature. Inefficiency can therefore be manifested in a
variety of ways in any project, all of them lowering the likelihood
of success.

A Case of Inefficiency

While overseeing a variety of residential and commercial construction projects, I faced the prospect of a major home renovation
shutting down due to permit issues. To keep a crew working, I
moved them to an office renovation. Unfortunately, the foreman
for the project fell ill and the crew went unsupervised for several
days. Upon visiting the site, I found that they had built less than
25 percent of the walls that were supposed to be complete by that
time, costing the company thousands of dollars. Watching them
work immediately revealed the problem. Because so-called "stick-
built" walls that use wood are often load-bearing, each stud has
to be saw-cut to exacting measurements to wedge into place for
nailing. In metal stud work (used in commercial renovation), the
walls are simple partitions that must bear only their own weight,
so the studs can be cut by hand, without as much precision. The
crew was meticulously cutting each stud to the perfect length
and fitting them in as if they were using wood, wasting an enormous amount of time on unnecessary quality.

Along with the monetary costs of lost time, the team had to be
retrained and driven hard to try to catch the schedule up. This
created hard feelings among the crew. Some of the walls had
been built so tightly that the studs actually bowed and had to be

reworked. Additionally, the residential job started back up and the crew had to be moved back to it before completing the office work. Finally, this inefficiency made both the foreman and me look incompetent.

Solutions

Although inefficiency can occur at any stage of a project (an obvious example is poorly run meetings), it can be especially costly during execution, when the bulk of the resource usage and expenditures takes place. Outside of directly observing the work being performed, which does not always yield meaningful data (and is not always practical, particularly in the case of knowledge work such as programming or process design), we must count on performance metrics to reveal inefficiency. Earned value management (EVM) is the gold standard for this, but it relies on mature project and financial management systems for implementation and does not begin to provide reliable measures until the project is 10–20 percent complete.

When change is forced onto a project, examine all standard processes for signs of potential problems. Don't let a project go without oversight for any significant length of time, particularly during periods of high expenditure or productivity.

Tips for Combating Inefficiency

▶ *At the beginning of a project, examine all processes for potential problems or waste.* Continuing to do something just because it was done in the last project is a sure way to foster inefficiency.

▶ *Leverage the best tools available for your planning process.* Although virtually all project planning can be performed manually, software provides enormous power for automation and what-if analysis.

▶ *Establish detailed baselines and use EVM for project reporting and control.* The proper use of EVM as a project control system ensures that corrective actions are taken only when necessary.

▶ *Maintain continuous review of the project with an eye toward waste and improvement.* Involve an outside project manager or agency to get a fresh set of eyes looking for inefficiency.

▶ *For every single activity, report, or meeting, ask "What would happen if I did not do this? What am I giving up in order to do this?"* Only through relentless examination of the opportunity cost for every action can we hope to make the best use of our most limited and precious resource, our time.

42

Inflexibility

Inflexible means immovable, unalterable; of a rigid or unyielding temper, purpose, or will. In project management, inflexibility can mean a personal preference for rigid structure and a tendency toward stubbornness. It can also refer to organizational models that aren't conducive to project management best practices.

The Sin

The sin of inflexibility can take two forms in the world of project management. The first form involves personal style and the interpersonal component of projects, and the second involves organizational cultural variables.

Personal style and the interpersonal component of inflexibility are apparent in the project manager or team member who typically has a structured, possibly rigid, manner of approaching the world. To use a common reference to illustrate this idea, consider the popular personality model, the Myers-Briggs Type Indicator (MBTI®). Those who have the MBTI® judging preference may pursue project completion and closure with such gusto that they run the risk of becoming inflexible to outside input. Judging personalities may communicate a disinterest in considering new ways of doing things, preferring to stick with procedures or technologies that are comfortable, or they may be short with others who express new ideas during meetings.

Inflexibility in project management is often evident during project crises, when individuals stick their heels in the ground, looking for comfort from tried-and-true problem-solving approaches or technologies that have served them well in the past. Physical fatigue or illness often brings out the inflexible in even the most open personalities.

Project inflexibility can also be part of the organizational culture. For example, some organizations or sponsoring executives claim to embrace project management methodologies, but in practice resist organizational models that allow project managers to share responsibility with functional managers (e.g., matrix organizational model). Instead they adhere to functional but rigid professional hierarchies that don't always facilitate project work.

Inflexibility often manifests itself on a project as important decisions being made away from team meetings, sponsoring executives offering a "yes, but" answer when confronted with resistance, and project managers appearing beleaguered and **powerless**.

A Case of Inflexibility

A number of years ago, a rapidly growing international technology company asked a consulting firm to help create an organizational development experience for its employees. The client wanted to enhance teamwork, promote social interaction among its employees, and generally increase levels of communication. The company had been founded by some very bright, technical subject matter experts who now needed to work more effectively interpersonally to stay abreast of the competition.

Unfortunately, the consultancy's project manager demonstrated inflexibility by believing that he knew best what the company needed (see **ego**), who should be involved in the planning process, and what the project deliverable should look like. He demonstrated his inflexibility by not listening well, not asking open-ended questions during team meetings, and expending a lot of effort to get other team members to agree that his plan was the best.

The result of this inflexibility was a series of organizational development efforts that did not really suit the client's organizational culture; as a result, its employees viewed the product as interesting but irrelevant to the issues they really faced. The client's senior management lost some respect (see **disrespect**) with employees, who wondered why the executives put them through these exercises when they had "real work" to do. Not surprisingly, the consultancy lost this client's subsequent business.

Danger Signs

Signs of inflexibility include not really listening to or working with other team members, such as **silence** during team meetings, late arrivals to or absence from meetings, and references to "your" program rather than "our" program. Other warning signs can come from individuals who do not seek input, insist on doing most of the work themselves, and resist integrating work contributions from multiple team members.

Solutions

Tendencies toward inflexibility can be a function of personal style, but that does not mean that individuals cannot change their behavior. The first step is self-awareness: Acknowledge tendencies to want to do something the same way each time or to resist any delay in getting the project completed. Second, ask sincere, open-ended questions to gain ideas and insights about new ways of operating. Third, be open to solutions and successes by other people—project responsibility does not have to rest entirely on one individual. And finally, gauge physical and emotional fatigue, as these can make people vulnerable to inflexibility.

Tips for Fighting off Inflexibility

▶ *Slow down, count to ten, and ask others what they think.* Asking questions with a genuine sense of interest and inquiry is a very effective way of being more flexible, both interpersonally and technically.

▶ *Recognize the ways that being flexible could benefit your career.* Recognizing the professional benefit of doing something can inspire you to try new things. There's nothing wrong with taking an appropriately selfish approach here.

43

Isolation

Isolation is setting or placing apart; detaching
or separating to be alone; keeping from contact
with others. Isolation can occur on many levels in
project management.

The Sin

Isolation in project management can take several different forms. Projects can be isolated from other projects that are being carried out within an organization. A project can be performed in isolation with regard to industry best practices, principles, or guidelines. Project stakeholders can be isolated from each other, and project managers can be isolated from the project team.

Projects often have artificial "walls" that lead to isolation (see **barriers**). Sometimes project teams build products, but not the products the client wants. Sometimes project managers fail to listen to the project sponsor. Sometimes they do not want to face reality and change the course of the project even in the face of evidence that the project is moving in the wrong direction. Isolation is sometimes caused by red tape, but it more often arises from common psychological biases.

People often believe in the superiority of their own decisions, even when faced with evidence that someone else has discovered a better path (see **not-invented-here**). We are reluctant to alter our plans even if the evidence suggests that we are heading toward **failure**. We fail to heed the advice of subordinates because we believe that because of our position, we are better able to judge the situation. All these factors can block the free flow of information in a project and lead to some form of isolation.

Isolation in turn leads to poor decisions based on wrong, inaccurate, or distorted information. The cost of wrong decisions can be enormous.

A Case of Isolation

Large, well-financed organizations often work in complete isolation. One multinational corporation needed to procure business analysis software. The staff briefly reviewed the software currently available on the market, determined that none of these software tools met their requirements, and decided to develop their own. The resultant project costs were far higher than the costs to license any of the third-party tools they had evaluated; even then, the software they developed failed to meet all their initial requirements. This organization was guilty of at least three common mistakes:

1. During their search for tools, they isolated themselves from the industry that produced the software. Searching Google is insufficient; the experts performing the evaluation must

not work in isolation, but must garner contacts to more fully understand the industry (e.g., vendors, requirements, capabilities).

2. They did not know that another division in their company had already developed an in-house solution for the same purposes. Their isolation caused them to spend a fortune not just once, but twice.

3. Some employees advised management that purchasing a commercial product was the best option. However, because they were working in isolation, management did not heed any recommendations that originated outside the management team.

Isolation can take many forms. In this case, isolation was caused by management's overconfidence in the company's ability to build a build a tool at a cost comparable to that of off-the-shelf software. First, they isolated themselves from the market by performing only a perfunctory evaluation of the existing commercial tools. Second, they isolated themselves from the opinions of their own experts when making the decision.

Danger Signs

One typical symptom of isolation is a lack of identified stakeholders. All internal and external stakeholders must be identified and documented. If the list of stakeholders appears to be thin or there is little documentation outlining stakeholder concerns, requirements, and related issues, this is definitely a symptom that the project team is working in isolation.

Signs of isolation must be diagnosed and addressed as early as possible; it becomes much more difficult and expensive to address problems as the project advances. It is a fairly well-known axiom in the software business that it is much less expensive to write the code properly than to address or fix issues later in the project.

Tips for Overcoming Isolation

▶ *Communicate, communicate, communicate.*

▶ *Set up processes so that all stakeholders are identified and engaged* in the project.

▶ *Engage outside consultants* to review your process and evaluate requirements if needed.

▶ *Minimize the size of your project team and use collaborative tools* to manage the project.

44

Lateness

Lateness is defined as coming or remaining after the due, usual, or proper time; tardiness; an advanced stage in time or development; deceased. Lateness in project management is typically understood as a project that is completed after the scheduled date identified in the project plan. Presumably, the scheduled date is determined according to a real or perceived customer need.

The Sin

Surveys of project management performance indicate that lateness is common across a variety of industries and organizations. The most common manifestation is the delivery of the specified product of the project after the scheduled date. However, because schedule is interdependent with scope/quality and resources, manifestations of lateness will appear in these elements as well. If a project runs late, stakeholders may agree to revise the deliverables or resources to accommodate the schedule. The project may deliver less and cost more than originally intended.

Where schedule is critical, being late may cause the complete **failure** of a project. An example could be as simple as missing a fixed deadline: A cake is worthless if it is delivered the day after a wedding reception. Often, commercial organizations with new product development projects must meet market "windows" to obtain an advantage over competitors. In such cases, failure to meet the scheduled window may cause complete failure or a dramatic reduction in profitability.

A Case of Lateness

Consider the TAURUS (Transfer and Automated Registration of Uncertified Stock) software project of the London Stock Exchange. The purpose of the project was to improve securities trading by streamlining transactions and making them more economical. Started in the 1980s, this effort was intended to make transactions paperless.

When the project began in 1986, it was scheduled to take three years and cost $11.5 million. By 1989, the project was sufficiently in trouble that the planned system was determined to be infeasible. Nevertheless, because of a recent stock market crash, it was decided that the TAURUS system was essential, and work continued. By 1993, the project was abandoned.

Because it was terminated, TAURUS is a great example of a project that fits the dictionary definition of *late* as "deceased"!

TAURUS stands out as one of the costliest failed IT projects in an industry known for troubled projects. It is estimated that the sunk cost of the project was $1.5 billion. This figure includes the costs incurred by the institutions that had invested in their own software projects to develop systems to be compatible with TAURUS as required by the stock exchange.

The final cost of the project was 130 times the original budget. Despite such an obscene cost overrun, in the end there was no software to show for all the effort and investment.

Danger Signs

A fundamental principle in project management holds that projects become late one day at a time. In other words, daily schedule **deviations** accumulate gradually, even though they may become "visible" only when tasks are not completed on time.

Stakeholders must beware of unrealistic optimism in the planning stages of a project, as well as at later decision points (see **magical thinking**). Prior to the TAURUS project, there had been several similar failed attempts in other countries. That knowledge alone should have led to an abundance of caution in the project plan. Even after three years of trouble, the stock exchange continued with the project because it was considered essential—without any realistic understanding of how it could be achieved. Termination of the project in 1989 would have saved enormous sums of money.

An owner or project sponsor can anonymously poll a number of knowledgeable yet independent people to obtain a sense of the likelihood of success. It is also helpful to anonymously poll project team members on their level of confidence in the achievement of project goals. A simple method involves asking each person his confidence level (e.g., 0–100 percent) in achieving project objectives with the baseline scope, schedule, and resources. When the average of a poll falls below 90 percent, or when individual answers are very low, trouble is likely in store.

The project core team has the greatest impact on schedule in the planning stage. If the core team is not realistic in the planning process, the schedule will start to slip right from the start.

Solutions

Since the TAURUS and similar project failures, many in the IT profession have become practitioners of better management methodologies. These include spiral development and agile techniques. Such methods are specifically designed to develop working software in shorter durations, with many more decision points. When such techniques are used, it becomes much less likely that a project will become late or even fall far behind schedule. These approaches help prevent a team from finding itself deep into a multiyear schedule, incurring huge costs with nothing to show for it.

It is also critical that each member of an organization think and act realistically in planning and executing projects. In many cases, individuals attempt to drive ill-advised projects without proper business justification. While a project manager may understandably have difficulty using it with an executive, the most underused word in the project manager's vocabulary is likely to be a simple "no." Failing to say no to unwise or unrealistic commitments is a fundamental reason why projects become late.

In essence, the difficulty with saying no is symptomatic of the difficulty with communication (see **miscommunication**). The solution to many issues related to lateness is open, honest, and proactive communication.

Remember that the project plan identifies the scope and quality of work, the resources or budget, and the schedule. These three elements interact to a significant extent throughout the project. Therefore, discussions of schedule and lateness must be conducted in the context of the project scope, quality, and resources.

Tips for Addressing Lateness

▶ *Make sure the scope of the project is divided into manageable pieces* with clear boundaries and interfaces.

▶ *Be obsessive about proactive and timely communication* on the project. Many project difficulties result from incomplete communication or incorrect **assumptions**.

▶ *Strive for honesty and realism* in project planning and reporting. By all means, it is critical that stakeholders know the true status of the project at any given time, not what is unrealistically optimistic.

▶ *Hold regular project reviews,* even brief ones, to check on schedule and to identify and resolve issues that impact schedule.

▶ *Time-box any task that involves ambiguity or uncertainty.*

45

Laziness

Laziness is aversion or disinclination to work, activity, or exertion, specifically the lack of desire to perform work or expend effort. This type of behavior is often attributed to human nature; its interpretation varies according to personal and societal standards. In the context of project management, laziness is the failure to willingly meet assigned performance requirements and obligations, in other words, irresponsibility.

The Sin

The larger the project, the more likely there are to be members of the project team with behavior problems, including laziness. On smaller projects, peer pressure tends to eliminate or reduce the impact of behavior problems, especially laziness, since all team members know each others' responsibilities.

Laziness manifests itself in team members missing deadlines or important coordination meetings, or ignoring emails or written communications regarding work on the project. Laziness and its symptoms are more likely to occur when there are no sanctions for not meeting responsibilities. An example is executive management's readiness to excuse overrun budgets or missed completion dates (see **excuses**). If performance requirements or goals aren't defined and emphasized, some project team members will reduce their effort.

When someone demonstrates that he is too lazy to do something, it's probably because that something seems boring or nonessential to him. The project manager or the person's supervisor must explain the importance of the project and the key role all team members play in its being carried out successfully.

A Case of Laziness

Lazy individuals do not normally gravitate toward projects but prefer positions that place fewer demands on their performance and are less stressful. The time, cost, and performance requirements of a project generally do not provide a comfortable environment for individuals with a tendency toward laziness.

We were working on a project related to improving the management processes within one of the major elements of the Smithsonian Institution. To get buy-in to the major recommendations, we held a day-long meeting with all the top-level managers, including the director. We were using a PowerPoint® presentation on a laptop and a projector to lead the group through the process. I had asked the person who was to handle the logistics of the presentation if she knew how to set up the system and she had assured us that she did. When it came time to use the projector system, it turned out that she had been too lazy to make sure everything was working and had in fact never set up a system before. We were embarrassed that we had to send the audience out on a break until we were able to get the system working. (This was not the first time she had exhibited lazy behavior, and a month later she was out looking for a new job.)

Danger Signs

Projects don't create laziness; individuals with a tendency to be lazy bring that trait to the project. On projects, the impact of laziness is seen in terms of costs, time, and morale. Costs are incurred when the lazy worker does not perform up to the expected and required level of production; therefore, the output of the project costs more in terms of person-hours than it should. With a lazy team member, it is likely that work will not be finished on time and that the work of others will consequently be delayed. Morale is affected because the other team members know when someone is not holding up his end of the work; if the project manager or the person's supervisor does not take action to address the issue, the impacts on morale and team cooperation can be far-reaching.

Solutions

There is really only one solution if you have a lazy person on the team: Talk to her and clearly describe the adverse events that will occur if the negative work habits persist —both to the project and, more important, to her personally.

To avoid having a lazy person on your team, the best course is to carefully check his background and experience prior to having him join the project team. Unfortunately, in matrix organizations, a project manager may be unable to do this. As soon as the lazy behavior becomes apparent, the project manager should report the poor performance to the individual's functional supervisor and request corrective action. Either the person's work habits will change or she will be dismissed from the project.

Tips for Confronting Laziness

▶ *Report lazy behavior immediately* to the individual's supervisor and demand corrective action.

▶ *Make it clear to the lazy team member what the consequences of this behavior will be.*

46

Magical Thinking

Magical thinking is the inaccurate belief that one's thoughts, words, or actions will cause or prevent a specific outcome even though that outcome does not reflect a realistic relationship between cause and effect. In project management, the relationships between cause and effect, planning and execution, and perception and reality are often lost. Magical thinking holds sway when management and customers harbor a belief that project managers can deliver despite known and recognized shortcomings in plans and allocated resources.

The Sin

Magical thinking abounds in most projects and is manifested a variety of ways:

▶ The stakeholders have unrealistic desires, estimates, and goals, leading them to place impossible demands and expectations on the project manager.

▶ Plans are made without any realistic steps for execution, as if the act of deciding on a direction will make it so.

- Budgets, schedules, and other plan components are recognized to be insufficient, but the project team is expected to proceed with the belief that it will all work out in the end.

- Lessons learned from previous projects are ignored when beginning new ones of a similar nature, and the heroic efforts that project teams had to make to succeed are overlooked (assuming that because things worked out last time despite the problems, they will work out this time as well).

A Case of Magical Thinking

On September 11, 2001, the worst disaster in the living memory of most citizens of the United States occurred with the destruction of the World Trade Center by terrorists in New York City. Even as the horrible aftermath of the event was being dealt with, options for rebuilding were being considered. Enormous amounts of input, time, effort, and money were devoted to selecting the design and planning for its construction.

The project to rebuild the World Trade Center is a perfect example of the costs of magical thinking. The construction of the replacement Freedom Tower was accelerated despite the complexities of the effort and the huge numbers of stakeholders involved. The cornerstone for the first design of the building was laid in July 2004, only to be removed in 2006 when security concerns forced a redesign. The original completion date of 2011 has moved to 2013, with no guarantees that further slippage will not occur. The original cost estimate for construction of the Freedom Tower was $2.2 billion, then $2.5 billion, and currently stands at $3.2 billion.

The magical thinking involved in this project has finally been recognized in a public fashion. "The schedule and cost estimates of the rebuilding effort that have been communicated to the public are not realistic," wrote Chris Ward, executive director of the Port Authority, which owns the site and is responsible for the biggest projects on it. "Indeed, it is time that the design of that complex project be made to conform to real budget and schedule expectations, which will require tough decisions that have not been candidly addressed up to now."

Danger Signs

Some of the early warning signs of magical thinking are easy to spot:

▶ Lack of a well-developed, rational business case for the project

▶ Nonexistent or inadequate chartering processes for the project

▶ Inability to determine the true business needs and interpret them into well-crafted project requirements

▶ Indefensible project plans created with no valid underlying processes (e.g., a schedule developed without a work breakdown structure, activity decomposition, or network diagram).

Solution

The solution to magical thinking is to follow established, proven project management processes (e.g., the Project Management

Institute's *Guide to the Project Management Body of Knowledge*) to generate realistic, defensible project plans. As a project manager, you should also practice continuous, proactive stakeholder management to ensure that magical thinking does not infect your projects. Finally, never accept a project that "smells bad" from the outset or appears impossible on its face.

Tips for Keeping Magical Thinking under Control

▶ *Address any disconnects between rational thought and irrational objectives* in the project selection and initiation stages.

▶ *Try to minimize the number of stakeholders involved* in project definition and design.

▶ *Break large programs down into tangible, more manageable smaller projects* and subprojects.

47

Malfeasance

Malfeasance is a legal term that refers to an individual intentionally performing an act that is illegal. In project management, malfeasance occurs when project managers or other stakeholders consciously manipulate or game project estimates to further their personal goals.

The Sin

Malfeasance is often the manifestation of the motivational biases of individuals or groups. These motivational biases cause stakeholders to distort the decision-making process to benefit their personal interests (financial or otherwise). Project planners often engage in this type of malfeasance by deliberately underestimating costs and overestimating benefits.

How do these motivational biases that lead to malfeasance actually occur? The figure below depicts a business represented by a triangle. In an ideal situation, businesses satisfy their clients who are willing to buy a product or service, which leads to an increase in the wealth of the owners and employees. This triangle represents the ideal balance in a system that is the foundation of the capitalist system. In reality, the objectives of any of the actors in this system can be achieved by other means. For example, the owners' and executives' short-term financial goals can conflict with the long-term goals of maintaining a healthy business relationship with their clients. Skewed objectives eventually lead to malfeasance.

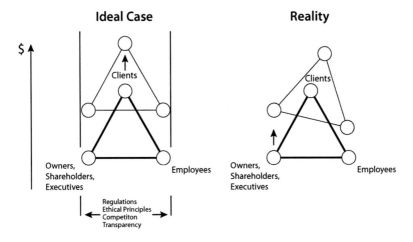

Conflicts of this type can lead to malfeasance, if the objectives of the three supporting sides of this triangle are wildly out of alignment and their motivations are particularly strong. For example, a company's executives are so strongly motivated to maintain their stock price that they are willing to sacrifice their long-term goal of maintaining a healthy business to meet this need. Often in these cases, a company will seek to improve its balance sheet by reducing expenses, primarily by laying off employees. However, when taken to the extreme, the executives may resort to forms of accounting shenanigans to meet their short-term goals (see **gaming**). In the long term, as the owners' objectives are met at the expense of clients or employees, the triangle becomes completely skewed and unstable.

A Case of Malfeasance

One well-known example of project management malfeasance occurred during the construction of the Chunnel, the railway tunnel connecting England and France. Eurotunnel, the private company that owns the tunnel, misled investors by understating the risk of cost escalation.

Eurotunnel originally estimated the costs of the Chunnel at 4.8 billion pounds. The final costs totaled 10.5 billion pounds, bankrupting Eurotunnel. Politically, the costs became a source of friction between the governments of Britain and France. Financially, the people most affected by the cost overruns of the Chunnel were the investors, which eventually came to include the British and French taxpayers.

Danger Signs

The motivational biases that underlie malfeasance are usually easy to identify, but they can be difficult to remedy. Understanding stakeholder interests is key to identifying where malfeasance might occur. What benefits does a project represent to each stakeholder? How are the stakeholders involved in developing project forecasts? If any of the stakeholders have an inordinate personal interest in the project, this must be taken into account in reviewing any information those stakeholders provide.

Solutions

All estimates for large or strategic projects must be reviewed by a party that has no interests in the outcome of the proposed project.

This can be difficult, as evidenced by the collapse of Enron, where supposedly disinterested auditors colluded with Enron executives to "cook the books." The malfeasance of the auditors occurred when they became dependent on Enron as a major source of revenue and were therefore no longer disinterested parties in evaluating the company's finances.

Tips for Avoiding Malfeasance

▶ *Ensure organizational transparency.* This requires more than simple disclosure of company financial information to shareholders. Employees, and in many case even clients, should know about the business' agenda, directions, and goals. In particular, project team members should clearly understand the project goals and objectives.

▶ *Encourage competition between different businesses and even project teams.* Competition will improve alignment of the objectives of the business, its employees, and its clients.

48 Meetingitis

Meetingitis can be defined as an excessive reliance on meetings to plan work (see **excess**), often at the expense of accomplishing actual work. The condition can be so severe that a person spends every part of the workday in meetings, one after the other. Anyone who has ever worked on a project can attest to the resulting fatigue, frustration, or burnout.

The Sin

Meetingitis is a well-known problem in project management. Project teams can spend hours in meetings without deciding anything or resolving any issues. This is unproductive and self-defeating. One common reason for meetingitis is a lack of clear objectives. Like Dilbert, we all experience meetings after which we think "what a waste of time this was"—while simultaneously agreeing to hold the same meeting the following week.

Meetingitis has three causes, which often occur in combination. The first is the project manager's well-meaning belief that all team members should be involved in every decision. The project manager sincerely believes that participatory management is the best approach and wants to make team members feel part of the entire project process.

A corollary to this all-inclusive approach is that team members value the participation of the project manager for her knowledge and for recognition and confirmation of what they are doing. That's a good thing, but one that can get out of hand.

The second source of meetingitis is that meetings spawn more meetings. Once calendars start to get crowded, everyone on the project learns the unstated rule: No work gets done except in meetings because there just isn't time outside of meetings.

Third, being in meetings can be seductive. For many staff, meetings represent a way of feeling important since they can be seen and heard by more senior managers. Similarly, project managers who need to confirm and reinforce their power view meetings as an opportunity to demonstrate their control to everyone.

Meetings have a real cost, which tends to be ignored. EffectiveMeetings.com has a meeting cost calculator that figures the annual cost of meetings. For example, the tool calculates that for a small company or project holding two-hour meetings with five people twice per week, the annual cost is $25,000.

Even more important, what about the cost in lost productivity? If a team member is totally engrossed in his work but needs to interrupt it to attend a meeting, there is an extra cost to consider: the time it will take to get back to the previous level of concentration.

Danger Signs

Many project managers fall into the trap of including all team members in every decision and meetings become project choke points. The big mistake is not empowering individuals with decision-making authority (see **no authority**). Many project managers give their staff some responsibility for collecting information and evaluating issues, but then fail to give them the power to make the decision. As a result, every decision, major or minor, is presented to the entire project team, often in a series of meetings.

Be alert to the tendency to convene meetings to analyze project information. When work that could be performed by individuals is instead performed by the project team, productive time is being lost.

Procrastinators often use meetings as a way to avoid getting their work done (see **procrastination** and **excuses**). Attending meetings, regardless of whether anything gets done, can create a false sense of accomplishment.

In the end, organizations that are consumed by meetings are usually organizations that are consumed by distrust. If the project manager doesn't trust the team members to make the right decision without his input, neither will anyone else.

A Case of Meetingitis

My worst experience with meetingitis was on a consulting project to the federal government that involved 30 engineers and scientists evaluating and developing a series of regulations. The regulations were grouped into four areas, so four subprojects were being conducted simultaneously, each supporting a different client organization. Decisions were being made daily. As the technical project manager with no formal project management training, I believed that project control and client inquiries about how the project was progressing required daily communication with each subgroup. I met with each subgroup for up to five hours each week to review staff efforts and analyses. I literally spent 50 percent of my time in meetings with project staff/managers and another 20 percent of my time communicating with the various clients. As a result, I had no time at work to get my own work done. I spent two or three hours every night at home working on my own deliverables and documents.

The pace was exhausting and. . .totally unnecessary. I had assigned very competent personnel to head each subgroup; they were good leaders, managers, and communicators. Each was well-liked by the staff under them. I was the problem: A lack of trust and project management experience caused self-inflicted demands for meetings that were too long and unfocused to be effective. The meetings never had an agenda or clearly defined objectives. Instead of using the meetings to build team cohesion, clarify expectations, identify issues, and stimulate creativity, we discussed every issue ad nauseum. Only through the heroic efforts of the subgroup managers, who worked even harder than I did, were we able to meet the clients' schedule and scope demands. In retrospect, if I had "treated" the meetingitis by trusting my subordinates, I could have enjoyed more time with my family —a true measure of success.

Tips for Eliminating Meetingitis

▶ *Set an agenda* before the meeting. Review the meeting objectives with attendees at the beginning of the meeting.

▶ *Delegate decisions* whenever possible. To minimize the risks of delegating, you will need to become very good at developing staff so they can excel (and feel confident) without your reviewing and approving every aspect of their work.

▶ *Be discriminating.* Choose which of the many meetings you actually need to attend. For the rest, delegate attendance to other members of your team, which serves the dual purpose of confirming your trust in them ("You know more about the subject than I do; I trust you to make the right decisions") and fostering staff interrelationships.

▶ *Make appointments with yourself.* Block out time in your calendar system. When the inevitable occurs and you need to use some of your reserved time for a meeting, schedule another appointment with yourself to make up for it.

49

Misalignment

Misalignment means improperly or incorrectly aligned; align means to bring into cooperation or agreement with a particular group, party, cause, etc. In project management, misalignment occurs when the goals or objectives of one working group do not match those of another working group, or when an organization pursues an endeavor that is inconsistent with its core competencies.

The Sin

Misalignment occurs when an organization is operating in ways that are incompatible with its stated strategy, goals, and objectives—a state that may or may not be apparent. Every project should align with the organization's strategic and operational goals and objectives. The more specific the goal or objective, the easier it is to ensure alignment.

Unfortunately, misalignment is fairly common, especially in organizations that handle cross-functional communication poorly. It is not uncommon for one project team to undertake a project that conflicts with the objectives of another project team in the same organization. Also, multiple functional units may be working on the same problem through concurrent projects.

A Case of Misalignment

Consider the space shuttle *Challenger* disaster. In 1986 the shuttle was destroyed when a booster failure caused an explosion, killing all seven astronauts onboard. This tragic accident was the result of several factors, some of which were associated with the misalignment of organizational goals and objectives.

The space shuttle program was meant to provide frequent and economical access to space via a reusable launch and reentry system. Despite its straightforwardness, multiple program objectives conflicted with this goal, and some of these misalignments contributed to the *Challenger* disaster. For example:

▶ To keep development costs low, Congress and the Office of Management and Budget reduced the funds allocated from original estimates of $10–$13 billion to $6.2 billion.

▶ NASA internal management needed to optimize resources to fulfill NASA's stated objective to provide frequent and economical access to space. In reality, this meant overextending resources to launch as many flights annually as possible.

▶ The contractor technical team was concerned about environmental operating conditions and external customer pressure.

Misalignments like these stretched the entire program to a breaking point. For example, the aggressive flight schedule included fewer shuttles and a reduced operational timeline between flights. Budget limitations resulted in a shortage of spare parts, which often led NASA to cannibalize or borrow parts from other shuttle systems. Reductions in the workforce led to long hours— overtime was typical, up to 28 percent in some instances.

Because of misalignment, program decisions were often based on incomplete or misleading information that conflicted with technical engineering data. NASA's program management structure bypassed certain shuttle managers, preventing decision-makers from learning about key technical issues and recommendations. In addition, project managers often felt more loyalty and accountability to their respective team than they did to the organization governing the entire shuttle program.

The Costs of Misalignment

The obvious costs of misalignment in the *Challenger* disaster were the tragic loss of the entire crew and the total destruction of the shuttle itself. In a project environment, misalignment often leads to distrust, poor decision-making, inefficient funding and budget decisions (see **inefficiency**), little or no accountability, increased risk, and unnecessary pressure on the project team. Priorities that are unclear or that constantly change divert attention from strategically important matters to "urgent" matters. These conditions stretch the project team and other resources to their limits, leading to burnout, low morale, and the loss of critical skills.

Misalignment during project initiation may cause management to focus on the wrong objectives, add unwanted projects into the portfolio, or burden internal resources. During project planning, misalignment can result in an imbalance of the classic competing demands of time, cost, scope, and quality. It is especially destructive if it's not identified until the later development or execution phases, because at that point the project has already expended valuable resources, likely depriving other projects of those resources.

Danger Signs

Signs of misalignment are not always obvious, but they are usually marked by arguments over resources, unclear priorities, uncertainty about the motivations behind a project, and a reluctance to make changes to the project portfolio—primarily because resource and portfolio managers don't know what their peers are doing and why.

If the priorities of one working group do not match those of another, self-protection and political coalition-building may become the norm. Look for indications that team members are focusing on local or tactical issues more than organizational or strategic issues. Also be aware of those who emphasize position instead of what is reasonable, logical, and practical.

When misalignment exists, working groups often fail to base project decisions on objective data; rather, stakeholders talk in broad, general terms, insisting on their own objectives and showing little interest in achieving a common goal. Some obvious signs of misalignment are bureaucratic roadblocks that reject certain goals as outside the working group's realm of responsibility (see **barriers**) and an insistence on maintaining specific operational capabilities even when doing so hinders cross-functional communications, decreases overall cooperation, or reduces system quality (see **shoddy quality**).

Lessons Learned

Misalignment will at the very least lead to the misallocation of resources and ineffective decision-making; at worst, it will lead to withheld or misrepresented project information and quality and safety shortcuts. Misalignment is often the result of inappropriate performance measures and control mechanisms. Without a comprehensive collaboration strategy that holds everyone accountable, functional groups and managers will feel no need to concern themselves with anything other than their own self-interests.

Tips for Correcting Misalignment

▶ *Remember that alignment is a shared responsibility* of all project team members and the management team.

▶ *Align all projects with the organization's strategic goals and objectives,* and periodically evaluate each project (and project decision) to ensure appropriate alignment.

▶ *Consistently—but appropriately—challenge project decisions, data, and processes.* Do not just blindly accept and implement them.

▶ *Ensure that all stakeholders understand the relationship and integration of all project components.* This will help maintain proper alignment by ensuring that everyone is working toward common objectives.

▶ *Establish and maintain a culture that emphasizes openness, honesty, and integrity.*

▶ *Implement mechanisms to improve communication and relationships* among the various stakeholders.

▶ *Create an atmosphere of cooperation, shared values, and mutual accountability* at all organizational levels to ensure that all decisions and actions align with what is best for both the project and the enterprise.

50

Miscommunication

Miscommunication is the failure to communicate clearly; it occurs when there is a disconnect between words and the message that was intended or received. In project management, miscommunication undermines the intentions of people at all levels and in all areas of the project. The inability to transmit information effectively, failure to listen and hear another person's intent, insistence on keeping things moving, predispositions, assumptions, and many other aspects of this complicated and highly personal behavior cause people to hinder and undermine each other's efforts.

The Sin

Miscommunication occurs on all projects to some extent; it is a natural and unavoidable by-product of working with others. Its manifestations on a project can be extensive, widespread, extremely destructive, and a root cause of project **failure**. The sin with respect to miscommunication is failing to work toward effective communication. Fortunately, the project manager can be proactive by demonstrating the critical importance of effective communication and providing the means to achieve it.

Often, projects provide too few mechanisms to foster effective communication. For example, most projects are composed of subgroups such as systems engineering, software development, quality assurance, configuration management, test, documentation, and training. One way to maintain effective communication on a project is for the project manager to sponsor regular brown bag presentations that facilitate and allow sharing of information. For example, the project manager could present topics such as customer concerns or project plans. An effective technique to maintain coordination within a project is to have each group present regularly concerning what it is doing. Training sessions can also be effective, as can rules of conduct (for example, arrive on time; respect others' viewpoints).

Another mechanism is to share "what's new since last week" among the project manager and the leads for each of the project areas. Things change rapidly on projects and people need to be made aware of the changes, react to them, reject them if needed (deferring the requested changes until a subsequent release, for example), and most important, manage them. People are unable to manage changes if they are not even aware of them.

A Case of Miscommunication

I was involved in a project where the customer provided the requirements specification to the project team. The team reviewed the spec and concluded that it was not adequate for them to design the requested system. They recommended to the customer that the spec be redone before design work began. The customer advised that its staff had spent two years developing the spec and insisted that it represented exactly what they wanted. The project team proceeded as directed and spent more than 50 person-years of effort working to design a system based on the specification. At the end of a year, the customer concluded that, yes, the spec needed to be redone—they had failed to identify the real requirements (see **poor requirements**).

The costs of this miscommunication included the 50 person-years of effort, an estimated one million dollars of customer and project expense, delay in providing needed functionality for users of the system, and human costs including low morale and high turnover associated with working on tasks that resulted in no benefit to anyone.

The project team obviously should have provided a better case in support of their recommendation to redo the requirements specification. For example, they could have noted deficiencies in the specification and provided examples of other design efforts that had failed because the real requirements had not been determined. A mechanism such as a vision and scope document can be used to develop the intent and objectives of a project, to determine what's in and what's not, to share that information among the people who are supporting the project, and to instill commitment to an understood set of project objectives.

Perhaps one of the most disrupting aspects of miscommunication is something project people refer to as "lessons learned." Lessons are usually observed, often reported on, but rarely learned (by individuals, project teams, projects, organizations, and nations). Lessons learned offer an opportunity to share aspects of previous projects that can save time, money, even lives—yet we fail to provide critical information to the right people. We need to be willing to invest time and effort to understand what has already been learned, to analyze and evaluate what should be done differently, and to apply the insights and knowledge on a new project in ways that overcome past errors.

Danger Signs

Signs of miscommunication on a project include:

▶ Frustration among participants in meetings.

▶ Concern that meetings aren't effective (see **meetingitis**).

▶ Individuals who insist that their idea, definition, suggestion, or approach is "right" (see **ego**)

▶ Misunderstandings among members of the project team

▶ Feeling of not having clear direction or guidance

▶ Making the same decision over again

▶ Lack of harmonious working relationships

▶ Having to do work over again ("rework")

▶ Surprises.

Solutions

The project manager should proactively address the topic of improving communication within the project. The team should brainstorm ideas for improving communication among project management, team members, customers, and major stakeholders. Developing a project glossary and acronym lists, so everyone is using a common vocabulary, is always a good idea. When making major decisions on projects, use a thumbs-up, sideways, or down mechanism: If anyone disagrees with a decision, ask what it would take to win her over and work to gain buy-in so that everyone can at least live with (thumb sideways) the decision. Without the commitment of the project staff to all key decisions made on the project, members of the team will not support each other fully, jeopardizing the success of the project.

Tips for Avoiding Miscommunication

▶ *Proactively address the topic of improving communication* on the project.

▶ *Brainstorm ideas for improving communication* within the project.

▶ *Agree on a common vocabulary.*

▶ *Gain the commitment of team members* to major project decisions.

▶ *Conduct regular information-sharing sessions.*

▶ *Provide training sessions.*

▶ *Develop "rules of conduct."*

51

Mismanagement

Mismanagement is incompetent or
dishonest management. In project management,
mismanagement is failing to use resources—
time, money, or people—properly.

The Sin

We always want our projects to come in on time, within budget, and according to the requirements indicated by the project's scope. Mismanagement means you are not allocating your resources correctly within the triple constraints and therefore your project will probably not be successful. New or inexperienced project managers are especially susceptible to mismanagement, or failing to use the proper processes. Often, project managers become overloaded with too many projects and are unable to direct adequate time to a specific project.

Mismanagement also occurs when a project manager does not fully or honestly communicate the status of the project to key stakeholders (see **miscommunication**). The project team, project leadership, and the customer are all told what they want to hear and critical resources either are not obtained or are kept long after they are needed.

A Case of Mismanagement

I worked on a large project that included both IT and business teams. This project had five project managers, all working under a senior project manager. Each was responsible for various components of the project. The senior project manager mismanaged the project resources in various ways:

▶ The project managers did not produce detailed project schedules.

▶ Project schedules were developed without input from the team, creating an unclear understanding of what the team could do and when.

▶ Some of the project managers were using the same resources—fully allocated to each subproject—because they didn't integrate project schedules.

▶ With no budget-to-actual reporting, the project managers would simply report that they were on track.

▶ When the project schedules fell behind, the project mangers were instructed to replan their project in a single day.

Needless to say, the project was out of control. We kept extending the timeline but without adequate project management processes and tools, the project managers kept making the same mistakes. The team members were burned out because they never saw any progress and the project was eventually canceled.

Danger Signs

Mismanagement begins when the project manager does not sufficiently plan, but it continues when the project manager does not properly communicate needs to leadership to obtain the appropriate resources. It gets worse when the project manager does not effectively monitor and control project activities.

Solutions

An easy way to understand how well a project is being managed is by using status reports. A good project schedule with planned and actual hours, as well as planned and actual costs, will show you when and where the project is out of control. Weekly or monthly reports showing how you are performing against the budget will allow leadership to keep a watch on how resources are being managed. Spending more each period than budgeted could indicate a problem with resource management.

Tips for Keeping Mismanagement from Destroying Your Project

▶ *Make time for detailed planning.*

▶ *Integrate plans for multi-layered projects* or programs.

▶ *Use standardized reports.*

▶ *Establish a baseline budget/schedule* and manage to it.

▶ *Communicate project progress* to key stakeholders.

52

No Authority

The dictionary defines authority as the power to decide or command. **No authority,** then, is the lack of power or inability to command. In project management, often the project's sponsor does not confer upon the project manager the authority to make decisions and take action; more often, the project manager is reluctant, unwilling, or incapable of exercising authority.

The Sin

The matter of authority—or lack of authority—speaks to the art, rather than the science, of project management. Not only must a project manager have the necessary authority, but the team must recognize and appreciate that authority. People will follow someone they believe will succeed. If the sponsor or organization does not grant authority to the project manager, that project manager has to step up and assert authority. No authority is not an **excuse** for failing to move the project forward and get results. An effective project manager is able to lead the team to success without formal authority.

An inherent challenge is that project managers don't own the resources they work with; team members are often drawn from other departments and report administratively to other managers. Even the project manager's own time is often matrixed and overallocated among various projects and departments. To run a successful project, the project manager must have the authority to obtain and maintain the necessary resources.

A Case of No Authority

I was involved with a project that covered a span of two years and involved a succession of three project managers. None of the project managers had the authority to move the project forward. Any one of them could have gone to the sponsor and addressed the need for authority—but didn't.

The sponsor claimed that the project was important to the organization and was high on the list of things that had to be accomplished. Even with this supposed commitment, however, team members were reassigned and two of the three project managers were pulled off to work on other projects in the organization—which spoke far louder than the sponsor's words (see **resource reallocation**). The third project manager was fired for being ineffective.

It is not easy to get authority when the sponsor is unwilling to grant it or is unaware that this is a problem. The sponsor in this case may have been pushing an agenda that the project manager was not privy to. Perhaps priorities changed, with other projects becoming more important strategically or having higher visibility for the organization. Regardless of the reason, the sponsor failed to empower the project manager. The project manager had no authority to get the project done in the context of the organization's hierarchical structure.

But, the project manager should have taken action and taken control—and created momentum for the project. He could have asserted to the sponsor, "You've given me this responsibility and said that this is your number one goal. Now, give me the resources I need to complete it." Project managers need to stand up for themselves and their projects—and make things happen.

Danger Signs

The indicators that there is a problem with authority often start to surface about six months into a project.

If the project manager waits to be told what to do next, there's a problem. She should have the authority to move the team to the next step.

If the project manager is waiting for personal approval from the sponsor, that too shows that he does not have the confidence needed to take the team in the right direction. It should be understood up front that the project manager does not have to wait for a go-ahead to take action.

If the project manager does not have authority to remove someone from the team, there's a problem. When a personnel change needs to be made, the project manager should be able to make it.

Solutions

Lack of authority is a common reason that projects fail, or drag on too long. A project manager's reluctance to take the leadership position may reflect a lack of self-confidence: Some people will never be comfortable wielding power. Leadership is one of those skills that can be difficult to learn as it is part of the art rather than the science of project management. The project manager needs to take advantage of training programs where basic leadership skills can be learned.

When the problem involves the sponsor, discussions need to take place. The team members, too, need to hold some authority. A masterful project manager builds **consensus** and leads.

The bottom line is that if you are not willing or able to move your team forward, for whatever reason, you should not be the project manager.

Tips for Demonstrating Authority over Your Project

▸ *Assert your authority.* If the sponsor says—or demonstrates—a lack of commitment to the project, find a way to assert authority and get things done.

▸ *Encourage team members to assert some level of authority.* If any team member delays delivering until directly asked by the project manager, that person is not taking full authority or responsibility for her job. The project manager should encourage team members to take control over their areas of responsibility on the project.

53

Not-Invented-Here

Not-invented-here (NIH) is a term used to describe a common type of organizational culture that resists accepting new ideas or innovations that have not originated within the organization. In project management, NIH is characterized by reluctance to use tools, templates, and processes developed outside the organization. As a result, the organization repeatedly reinvents the wheel, unnecessarily creating its own tools, templates, and processes—often at much greater costs.

The Sin

A reluctance to consider tools, templates, and processes developed by others typically stems from the belief that because the organization's environment, products and services, customers, etc., are unique, adopting a tool or practice from any other source simply will not work. It may also be a symptom of an organizational resistance to change or to something new or different.

By definition, every project is unique. However, because every project has common elements, it is often possible—and advantageous—to identify best practices and existing tools and techniques and tailor them to fit the particular needs of the project.

An NIH attitude places artificial **barriers** around the project, hindering the team's ability to succeed.

The NIH attitude is more common in project management than many are willing to admit. The attitude is prevalent in organizations that pride themselves on their problem-solving abilities, innovativeness and creativity, and self-reliance—such as research and development (R&D) organizations, engineering firms, level-of-effort environments, and academia. Project environments that reward creativity over efficiency or emphasize billable time over effectiveness are more inclined to adopt the NIH attitude as a standard practice.

Sometimes the NIH attitude stems from ignorance: Business unit A may have a tool, template, or process that business unit B could use, but unit B doesn't know what unit A has to offer and doesn't realize that it might be worth inquiring about. This ignorance might be the result of ineffective communication systems (see **miscommunication**), inexperience, or simply an unwillingness to consider different approaches to a situation (see **blinders**).

A Case of Not-Invented-Here

ABC Corporation is a large manufacturing company that produces consumer electronics for retail sales and specialized products for military applications. ABC has a typical organizational structure with the classic functions—R&D, engineering, manufacturing, sales and marketing, human resources, etc.

In an effort to manage costs and increase profitability, ABC management decided to streamline its product development and commercialization process by implementing a standardized project management methodology. The company established a training program, identified some basic templates and tools to apply throughout the company, and purchased a well-known stage-gate methodology.

Trouble emerged on the very first day of training. Class attendees declared that the course content could not be applied to their unique departments. For example, attendees representing the organization's R&D group claimed it was impossible to plan a schedule or estimate a budget for first-level research; the operations support staff insisted that because all their projects begin as last-minute requests, they have their own way of tracking projects.

Departments throughout the organization pushed back against the new project management methodology and tools because the components did not completely fit their unique needs. Following training, employees rarely used the new templates, reverting to basic spreadsheets and word-processing tools to manage projects. They continued to make project decisions on a crisis-management basis.

The pervasive NIH attitude caused ABC to waste resources, disrupt profit-generating activities, and lose opportunities to achieve project objectives efficiently (see **inefficiency**). NIH can also negatively affect communications and team building when it requires other stakeholders to change their processes to accommodate the NIH organization. Over the long term, employees often experience frustration and in-fighting because of their organization's overemphasis on its uniqueness. In reality, the NIH attitude is simply another form of **ego** and pride.

Costs of Not-Invented-Here

NIH can be costly throughout a project, but it is typically most obvious and troublesome during the project initiation and planning phases, when the basic framework for the project is defined. During project initiation, stakeholders identify a problem and agree on the best alternative for solving that problem. If stakeholders—including the project team—consider only internal options, they may overlook more viable alternatives.

During project planning, the team works to determine the tools, techniques, processes, and procedures that will be used during the project. An NIH attitude during project planning is likely to limit the effectiveness of these project management resources; it can cause project managers to neglect useful tools or sound input from other team members, creating **confusion** and frustration among stakeholders.

Danger Signs

If an organization reacts to the need for a new tool, technique, or process by focusing on only what the organization has internally without considering outside resources as potential alternatives, it might have an underlying NIH culture. Some phrases commonly associated with the NIH attitude include:

▶ "We're different."

▶ "It won't work here."

▶ "That's not how we do it."

▶ "If you want it done right, do it yourself."

Look also for employees who appear to be working against the organization's overall goals and objectives. In other words, look for employees who focus more on achieving personal objectives by creating something new from scratch, regardless of the resources it will require or its potential impact on quality (see **shoddy quality**). Also be aware of anyone who appears to encourage others to speak negatively about using an external solution, especially if that alternative pushes the organization in a direction that goes against a long-standing cultural norm or common practice.

Solutions

Outside resources rarely fit an organization's unique needs perfectly, but this shouldn't prevent organizations from adopting and tailoring resources when appropriate to avoid continually reinventing the wheel. And keep in mind that developing something from scratch doesn't guarantee a perfect solution or eliminate potential problems, either.

People usually resist unnecessary change. An organization must give employees a compelling reason to eliminate their NIH attitude. Companies rarely reward the appropriate integration of best practices that originated elsewhere. Instead, they focus on developing proprietary tools, techniques, and processes, regardless of the cost.

Management has the responsibility to establish and maintain an internal system that ensures that best practices from one business unit are visible and are applied to other units as appropriate. Management must hold its employees accountable for applying best practices on their projects, regardless of the origin of those practices, and they must ensure that information about best practices is readily available. If not, counterproductive behaviors like NIH will continue.

Tips for Addressing a Not-Invented-Here Attitude

▸ *Encourage team members to leverage resources* from within the company as well as from outside sources.

▸ *Challenge them to consider viable solutions* or alternatives available from outside sources.

▸ *Reward team members for identifying cost-effective solutions and best practices* from external sources.

▸ *Consider custom development as the option of last resort.*

▸ *Establish a checklist or criteria to determine if internal development is the most cost-effective alternative.* Incorporate these criteria into the project initiation and planning phases.

▸ As part of project closure, *require team members to document best practices.* Ask them to identify other business units that might benefit from those best practices and propose a logical way to transfer the information.

▸ *Acknowledge that moving beyond an NIH attitude will require a culture change,* typically at all levels of the organization. Begin by focusing on what can change at the project level or within other areas of your control.

54

Obtuseness

Obtuseness is the quality of being slow to understand;
a poor ability to understand or to profit from experience;
lacking sharpness or quickness of sensibility or intellect;
not clear or precise in thought or expression.
It often seems that obtuseness just can't be avoided
in project management.

The Sin

Obtuseness has multiple sources and seems to plague most projects. In fact, one could argue that obtuseness is what good project management practices are designed to address.

Obtuseness can surface in people: the customer, the sponsor, the project manager, the project team, and other stakeholders. It can be also be found in the project work itself as a result of the failure to use sound project management processes, tools, and techniques.

Think for a moment about the common problem of unclear project requirements received from a customer (see **poor requirements**). A skilled project manager can respond successfully to this lack of clarity and elicit more precise requirements. But what happens when the project manager is slow to understand that she is embarking on a project that is riddled with ambiguity—that this project is likely going to take longer, cost more, and not be what the customer had in mind?

Then, of course, there is always that one project team member who believes he knows everything and is insensitive to input from the other team members; he loves to hear himself talk and always believes he has the only solution or idea in the room (see **ego**). To avoid a mutiny, a strong project manager must provide very specific feedback to this person and the team must actively enforce its ground rules.

Obtuseness is to be expected on projects that are cross-functional or cross-cultural. These projects often inherently suffer from clarity issues arising from the various perspectives the team members bring to the table. The team will need to acknowledge and work on this "legitimate" obtuseness throughout the duration of the project.

Underestimating or failing to recognize the value of using lessons learned is a key aspect of obtuseness, reflecting "a poor ability to understand or to profit from experience." Ignoring the experiences of others is **shortsighted** and wasteful, to say the least.

A Case of Obtusenesss

I worked on a project primarily as a functional manager stakeholder. The overall project was to outsource the "simple" sales, sales support, service, and billing functions from the company's customer service center and billing department. This telecommunications company, located in a major metropolitan area, decided to move these functions to a company located in a fairly remote part of a midwestern state. Labor rates would be significantly lower there and the sponsor believed that anyone could learn the sales, service, and billing functions for any type of industry relatively quickly.

The project was to be completed in phases by transitioning the less technical functions first, allowing the newly trained customer service representatives time to get acquainted with the industry, product line, and well-informed commercial customers. The vendor's prior experience had been with taking reservations for hotels, receiving orders for flower delivery, and handling newspaper delivery complaints—not at all the technical kind of work it would be doing on this new project.

New tasks were transitioned on a very ambitious project schedule that had been dictated by the sponsor, with virtually no input from the project manager, functional managers, or new vendor (see **close-mindedness**). The sponsor didn't listen to or include any input provided to the project plan or schedule, partly out of arrogance and partly because of a failure to understand the nature of the work.

No one was happy, from the project sponsor to the customer service representatives. The sponsor was upset that milestone dates were being missed and additional staff had to be hired to handle the growing call volume; the customer service representatives were resentful of the constant criticism from the sponsor and the customers. The project manager and team didn't know which fire to put out first—the schedule dictated everything.

The costs of this very challenged project were significant. Despite the sponsor's attempts to strictly enforce the project schedule, tasks and activities took much longer than planned (see **lateness**) and were not completed accurately. Budgets were overrun. Frequent business trips were necessary for the staff to provide additional on-site training and technical support. Turnover was extremely high and morale very low. The vendor considered legal action because of numerous contract issues.

This all could have been avoided had the sponsor not been so obtuse, if he had listened to the input from the project team and the vendor. He clearly didn't use much of the readily available data and experience from his project team before or after launching the project. His obtuseness basically sank the project from the get-go.

Tips for Combating Obtuseness on Your Project

▶ *Escalate to a higher level of authority* when a project is going down the wrong path. Have your facts and bring recommendations to those higher-ups. You will be glad you did and you will likely be thanked when all is said and done.

▶ *Recognize when project requirements are unclear* and resolve those ambiguities as quickly as possible.

▶ *Be very conscious of when business, functional, and or cultural differences inherently bring obtuseness into a project.* Hold meaningful team sessions to clarify and appreciate those differences.

▶ *Establish some good, clear team ground rules* and ensure that they are enforced. Initiate those sometimes tough but necessary conversations with team members who are violating the ground rules.

▶ *Conduct "lessons learned" sessions* at the completion of each phase of the project or even at the end of a mid-phase event that worked particularly well or had problems. Don't wait until the end of the project.

55

Omission

Omission is the act of neglecting to perform an action one has an obligation to do. In project management, omission means neglecting to perform any task that is required to produce and deliver the end product or service of the project.

The Sin

In project management, omission manifests itself in two categories: things we don't do and things we can't do.

First there are the things we don't do. Here, tasks are omitted because we:

▶ Failed to plan ahead sufficiently or to think past the issues immediately at hand

▶ Procrastinated, focusing on the easier, more "fun" things to do (see **procrastination**)

▶ Did not perform the necessary preliminary steps

▶ Simply failed to recognize the items that were omitted—we did not dig sufficiently for appropriate levels of detail when we thought we were analyzing the requirements (see **poor requirements**).

And then there are the things we can't do, because:

▶ Someone, or some rule or statute, precludes their accomplishment

▶ Budgetary or time constraints prevent their accomplishment

▶ The wrong resources, or not enough resources, have been assigned.

Omission is most costly at critical stages of the project. For example, if the testing of the deliverable reveals major flaws, the project team will need to go back to the drawing board and figure out what was omitted. Even worse, if the deliverable does not perform as it should after being delivered to the customer, the customer must take the time to request a fix—and might even refuse to use the product or service (see **shoddy quality**). In this case, all the money and time that were devoted to the project were wasted.

A Case of Omission

I once helped a newly formed software firm with a project to develop a "killer app." The firm was well behind schedule to release the software as announced. The team's morale was very low; the team members felt they were constantly spinning their wheels on this evident "**failure**."

When I looked at their plan, I saw that they were using a time-oriented work breakdown structure (WBS): preliminary design, detailed design, code and unit test, integration test. The team members were puzzled because they were following the WBS they had established, yet they were not achieving the goals of the project.

I got the project team to redo the WBS based on the functionality of the software they were trying to produce. We put design tasks at every level of every module of the functional structure and then put test tasks everywhere that we had design tasks. It quickly became evident that many design tasks were not completed, even though a design document and review had been completed. We also saw that many integration test tasks could be accomplished but were being held up because of the "boxed-in" structure of the schedule.

The omission of many of the design tasks had created numerous problems for the team in trying to determine how to write the code so it would work with other functions in the modules. Additionally, the delay of the testing tasks that could be accomplished created the risk that some of those tasks would be "omitted" due to time constraints. The introduction of a new, deliverable-oriented WBS structure allowed the team to focus on what had been omitted up to that point and to mitigate the future omission of the testing activities.

Once the focus changed, the project team's morale improved immensely. The software released on time and not as far over budget as it could have been.

Danger Signs

If problems arise during testing of the deliverable, it is likely that significant tasks were omitted. Consider the testing problems a warning that the project manager and team need to take a careful look at whether and how the processes of initiating, planning, executing, and controlling have been carried out on the project.

Solutions

Omission is an inevitable risk. We can't guarantee that all things in every project will be defined, analyzed, and specifically planned, so as not to be omitted. Going back to the definition of omission, the operative word is "neglect."

However, we can mitigate the risk. It is critical that the project team members learn the project management processes that must be followed to plan the project well. If all the processes of initiating, planning, executing, and controlling the project are performed well, no aspect of the project will suffer from neglect and the risk of omission will be minimized.

Tips for Keeping Omission from Derailing Your Project

▶ *Take sufficient time to analyze the requirements* of the project.

▶ *Document the scope of the deliverable* in a detailed deliverable-oriented work breakdown structure.

▶ *Involve the customer* in this design/planning process.

▶ *Acquire sufficient resources* to carry out all the tasks required.

▶ *Balance the project scope to the budget, time, and resources.*

▶ *Measure and monitor* the progress of the project.

56

Opposition

Opposition is a person or group objecting to or
working against a proposal or plan. In project
management, opposition refers to an individual or
group resisting change in general or resisting the
specific change brought on by the project.

The Sin

Opposition can be understood in the context of a project as a
stakeholder who is either against the project overall or against
some specific approach or detail on the project. At the very least,
this individual's actions or attitudes act as an obstacle to the
project (see **barriers**) and have the potential to promote a hostile
atmosphere.

Opposition is common on projects. Not all opposition is bad,
however. When a project manager discovers opposition, he or
she should first attempt to determine if it is warranted. Perhaps
the stakeholder has a good reason that needs to be considered.
When the project manager listens and makes changes based on

legitimate opposition, the project plan is often improved and the project has a higher probability of success.

The "sin" of opposition occurs when someone resists a project beyond the point of refining the plans. When this opposition is overt, it can be openly discussed. When the opposition is hidden, it is more difficult to address. First, it is hard to overcome something unless you know it exists. Second, by the time the opposition becomes known, it may be so late in the project that the project manager's choices for how to deal with the opposition may be more limited. If the opposition is insurmountable, the project may fail. More often, the opposition limits project choices.

A Case of Opposition

We were reengineering our entire MBA program to make it fresher and more current. This was an important project for the university but we did not view it strictly as a project and, we later realized, we therefore neglected to establish the framework necessary for a successful outcome.

Our MBA director served as the sponsor. It was important that the sponsor speak with a number of the faculty members from each department early in the process to get a sense of whether the plan to reengineer the program was likely to meet with a great deal of opposition.

Working in a collegial setting, we did not name a project manager. We considered all representatives equal so no department would feel slighted (see **no authority**).

One department sent a representative who refused to consider any changes to the courses taught by his department. The representative said that his department was totally opposed to making any changes. As time went on, the representative gradually became willing to make some concessions. However, we later discovered that the other members of his department had not agreed to these concessions.

Belatedly this department decided that since all the other departments had exciting new courses, perhaps they were missing out. At the eleventh hour, they decided they should make some cosmetic changes. In the end, this department's curriculum was changed for what most people thought was the better.

Had it not been for the opposition from one department, the project could easily have been completed as much as a year earlier, giving us a competitive advantage over other university programs. Another big cost was in the bitter feelings that were engendered between various individuals and departments.

Each stakeholder, in this case each department representative, should have been capable of expressing the views of the stakeholders he or she represented. The department representative also should have had the ability to persuade the members of the department that decisions that were laboriously made by **consensus** were really good decisions for the entire group and should be supported. Naming a project manager might have made the entire process easier and more effective.

Solutions

If the project team is at an impasse, with different groups of stakeholders unwilling to budge, new options should be formulated. The representatives from the various stakeholder groups need to be able to think creatively and collaboratively to develop options that may meet with less resistance (see **blinders**).

Perhaps the more important work needs to be done first. That is, all the stakeholders need to be aligned with the overall project goals (see **misalignment**). When a significant issue arises, there should be open discussion regarding the "elephant in the room." One of our problems at the university was that quite a few tenured professors (who were powerful stakeholders) did not truly believe that we needed to change. Although our program was successful, the dean was saying the wolf is next door, then the wolf is at the door, then the wolf is at the table.... These stakeholders needed to be convinced of the need for this project.

Another idea is to treat the opposition as the first step toward resolution. Expressing differences openly allows a **conflict** resolution process to begin.

All stakeholders need to feel they are part of the team. Yet, every team needs a leader—a project manager. Everyone does not need to feel exactly equal, but everyone needs to buy into the project and feel they are part of the team.

Finally, both the sponsor and the project manager need to try hard to have all stakeholders value each other. In a university setting, professors from quantitative disciplines often do not value what those in behavioral disciplines teach and vice versa (see **disrespect**). On many projects, some stakeholders feel their needs are more important than others (see **ego**). The sponsor and the project manager need to take steps to make sure that these attitudes do not derail the project.

Tips for Addressing Opposition

▶ *Name a project leader.* No matter how informal the project is, it should have a leader.

▶ *Identify opposition from stakeholders.* If an individual or group opposes the project, find out at the earliest point in the process. Opposition won't lessen with time.

▶ *Align stakeholders with the project goals.* Stakeholders who understand and agree with project goals are likely to offer constructive opposition that makes the project better rather than destructive opposition that may hinder project success.

57

Politics

Politics is the use of strategy and intrigue in obtaining power, control, or status; the practice of engaging in behavior or conducting activities to exercise or seek power. Projects, like life, are rife with politics. As Albert Einstein noted, "Politics is more difficult than physics."

The Sin

Strategic projects are by their very nature politically sensitive. Highly visible projects involve the most powerful and influential people, creating complex organizational and interpersonal situations. Major change brought about by projects almost always destabilizes the existing power structure, prompting unpredictable behaviors at senior levels of the organization. Moreover, every organization has undefined political processes and ever-present power struggles. Political maneuvers can be stifling and overwhelming to a project—if not managed, they can lead to project **failure**. To survive, much less succeed, project managers and leaders must be aware of and adapt to political events as they occur. Strategies can shift, causing virtually every aspect of a complex project to change. Project stakeholders often have changing expectations. Relationships with executive stakeholders create political complexity, as do hidden management expectations.

In the context of project management, politics has several dimensions:

▶ *At the project or program level*—between members of the project team or across multiple teams within a program.

▶ *At the organizational level*—usually focused on the acquisition of power. The internal structure of an organization continually deals with power and influence, positive or negative, to resolve **conflicts** and to achieve organizational or personal results. Since projects are conducted within organizations, organizational politics is always in play.

▶ *External to the organization*—within the community of stakeholders such as state and local governments, suppliers, clients, and customers.

Politics can have both positive and negative impacts on a project. To manage the political challenges, the project manager must have the ability to deal with complex organizational entities and interpersonal situations. This requires project managers to be politically astute and to have effective interpersonal skills (the so-called "soft skills") like conflict resolution, problem-solving, and negotiating.

In addition, strong executive support is crucial to the success of complex, politically charged projects, particularly if those projects are highly visible.

A Case of Politics

During the 1980s and early 1990s, the chairman of a major player in the food and drug industry acquired many regionally owned food and drug stores. He then launched the largest reengineering project in the U.S. retail industry to bring all the regional companies onto one IT system with common business practices. About 100 of the best and brightest young managers were brought together to serve as the reengineering team. An IT staff of about 150 was recruited. A consulting firm was hired to facilitate sessions to determine the future state of the business practices. The same consulting firm committed to scaling up its current supply-chain IT system and to ensuring that it met the requirements generated by the reengineering team. The plan was for all the regional companies to become one company and thereby leverage their purchasing power.

The project was visible at the highest levels of the organization: It was about their future. The CFO reported progress to Wall Street on a quarterly basis. As a result, the project was subject to political power struggles at every turn.

The business case was considered sound and promised to return huge profits (see **promises**); however, the project was never able to execute against the projections in the business case. The reasons were many and varied but were rooted in political power struggles. The project leadership team was made up of managers who had been very successful in the retail industry, but who had no experience leading highly complex projects. As a result, senior vice presidents vied for power and control. Vital resources who were trying to organize the project were cast aside by the leadership team. Information was hoarded. **Consensus** was virtually nonexistent. The project leadership was changed often, hoping to strike a better balance. The project resources were divided down the middle (physically and emotionally) between the information technology group and the business team—a divide that was not to be crossed (see **resource reallocation**). Key stakeholders were ducking for cover as the project began to unravel. Meanwhile, the industry was becoming even more competitive.

Five years into the project, the company was bought out by a competitor. Hundreds of millions of dollars had been spent and nothing had been implemented.

Danger Signs

Several warning signs indicate that politics is causing **dysfunctional** behaviors on project teams:

▶ A project manager who is making decisions unilaterally, without involving critical stakeholders

▶ A project manager who has the trust of senior business managers and uses this relationship to discredit the views of critical stakeholders

▶ Conflict on managing requirements scope and priorities among the stakeholders

▶ An opposing approach to managing changes to requirements among critical stakeholders

▶ Inability on the part of the team to secure decisions from project sponsors, thus adversely impacting forward progress.

Solutions

Developing a *political management plan* can help you anticipate and preempt political risks that may adversely impact your
project. To develop this plan, start by conducting an assessment
of the political landscape, including the stakeholders, the environment, your political capabilities, and the political risks.

Step 1: Assess the Project Stakeholders

1. Identify the individuals who:

   ‣ Oversee the project

   ‣ Provide input to the project

   ‣ Receive output from the project

   ‣ Have related responsibilities

   ‣ Benefit from its success

   ‣ Suffer from its success.

2. Assess each stakeholder according to his ability to assist or
   block the success of the project:

   ‣ His support is not necessary now

   ‣ It would be helpful to have his support

   ‣ It is critically important to have his support.

3. Measure each stakeholder's existing or expected level of
   support for you and the project:

   ‣ Actively supports the project

   ‣ Is neutral to the project

- Opposes the project and may work against it
- Level of support unknown.

4. Identify the issues and concerns regarding the project that are important to each stakeholder:
   - What's in it for her?
   - What does she need to view the project positively and actively support it?

5. Determine the best strategy to influence the stakeholder.

6. Identify a contingency plan if that strategy fails.

Step 2: Assess the Environment

- Is the business case solid?
- Is the project politically sensitive?
- What are the unspoken expectations?
- What is the decision-making process?
- What is the political culture?

Step 3: Assess Your Political Capabilities

How well do you:

- Enlist the help of an executive sponsor?
- Organize and chair a project oversight committee?
- Make yourself an expert?
- Promote yourself and your project?
- Manage project benefits?
- Manage virtual alliances?

▶ Facilitate, negotiate, and build consensus?

▶ Manage conflict?

▶ Develop a political management strategy?

Step 4: Assess Your Political Risks

▶ Organizational risks

▶ Environmental/organizational issues

▶ Extent of change the organization is undergoing

▶ Political games/maneuvers

▶ Stakeholder risks

▶ Work to lessen the impact of those who may negatively influence the project

▶ Enlist the help of those who are positive about the project

▶ Be aware of the "what's in it for me" mentality

▶ Capability risks—your ability to:

  ▸ Build relationships

  ▸ Manage conflicts

  ▸ Facilitate consensus

  ▸ Develop a political management strategy.

Step 5: Develop Your Political Management Plan

Establish plans to:

▶ Negotiate the environmental land mines

▶ Manage stakeholders' influence

- ▶ Develop your political skills

- ▶ Respond to political risks

- ▶ Develop risk response strategies

- ▶ Continually evaluate and fine-tune your approach.

Tips for Making Politics Work for Your Project

- ▶ *Collaborate with the business analyst, lead technologist, business visionary, and all other core team members* to conduct a political assessment and develop a political management plan.

- ▶ *Secure and maintain executive-level support* by enlisting the help of a strong executive sponsor, establishing a steering committee, and focusing on business benefits.

- ▶ *Involve customers and users* in every aspect of your project.

- ▶ *Continually validate* the effectiveness of your political management strategies.

- ▶ *Never compromise* your integrity and honesty.

58

Poor Planning

Poor planning can be defined as the lack of an organized and timely approach to complete a task. In project management, poor planning manifests itself as the inability to define the entire scope of the work to be performed and the tasks required to complete the work.

The Sin

All too common in project management, poor planning typically first becomes evident during the execution or delivery stage of a project. Poor planning can occur for many reasons, including lack of knowledge about how to properly plan a project; lack of knowledge about how to develop a work breakdown structure (WBS) and baseline project schedule; lack of experience and understanding of the work to be performed; insufficient funding and time allocated for planning; having the wrong resources and skill sets plan the project; and inability to draft a quality statement of work (SOW).

It is often not until the execution or delivery phase of the project that poor planning is recognized. Unfortunately, this is also the most costly stage to recognize that the project was poorly planned. At this point, work often has to be stopped to go back and do the proper planning. Any delays or stoppage of work equates to dollars being lost on the project. In some cases the project may proceed while a change order is processed for additional work that may be required. This, however, will also equate to additional funding beyond what was originally budgeted to complete the project. The cost of change is always lower at the beginning of a project and increases significantly as the project moves closer to completion.

A Case of Poor Planning

One of the first and most easily recognized cases of poor planning that I witnessed occurred on a large IT outsourcing project in which a contract had been negotiated and signed with a client without any detailed planning being conducted. Rather than undertake a detailed planning effort for the work, the service provider opted to simply draft a five-page SOW: four pages of résumés and one page describing the work to be performed. As you might guess, this one-page description of work was not based on a detailed WBS, but instead was simply a narrative description of what the executive leader for the service provider thought she could deliver on the project.

Without having conducted a detailed planning analysis, the service provider made commitments to the client that they could not deliver on. In addition, service level agreements (SLAs) were signed that had financial penalties associated with them if the service provider did not deliver on time. As a result of its lack of planning on this project, the service provider was unable to adequately deliver the services to the client and incurred significant financial penalties—approximately $50,000 per month. No surprise, the client was not satisfied with the work performed. Fortunately, the client was willing to renegotiate the contract and allow the service provider to conduct a detailed planning effort that took into account the entire scope of the work to be performed, which had initially been overlooked.

Once the project was reinitiated, the service provider was able to meet the SLAs for the project and to deliver the work successfully to the client. This project eventually became a very profitable engagement for the service provider. The additional planning effort turned a failing project into a success story.

Danger Signs

One of the best ways to recognize the sin of poor planning on a project is by the number of change orders being submitted. Change orders are a clear indicator that the entire scope of the project was not adequately defined and all the tasks required to deliver the work were not properly identified. One of the ways to screen for this sin is to involve the team members responsible for delivering the work, as well as the client, in developing the WBS, the schedule, and the SOW for the project. Collaborating with the client or end user in this process will greatly reduce the likelihood of poor planning.

When SLAs have been established but are not being met, this is also a clear indicator that adequate planning has not been conducted on the project.

Tips for Planning Well

▶ *Ensure that adequate time and funding are allocated* to properly plan a project.

▶ *Involve the correct resources and skill sets* in the planning process.

▶ *Train project team members* on how to properly plan a project and draft a quality SOW.

▶ *Include the client or end user* as part of the team during the planning stage of the project.

▶ *Be knowledgeable and have the competencies* to completely understand the work that is to be planned and delivered.

59
Poor Requirements

A requirement is a need or necessity, something obligatory. In project management, a requirement is a clear statement of that need, sufficiently detailed that there is no question about what is being said. **Poor requirements** leave the development team without a clear understanding of what the final product should be.

The Sin

The goal of the project manager is to deliver the product the customer expects, within schedule, cost, and quality constraints. The product itself is defined by the requirements provided by the customer. As project managers, we don't own the requirements—our customer owns them and can change them—but we are fully responsible for fulfilling them.

Everything we do on the project is defined by the customer's product requirements. The schedule is built around our ability to satisfy them with the resources we have. The budget tells us how much it will cost to develop the final product. A significant body of research in many fields shows that missing or poorly stated requirements can have a significant impact on both the cost of the project and the delivery date.

In the construction industry, the building owners determine the initial requirements. The architect then designs a building that meets those requirements and the engineering team takes the architectural drawings and creates the engineering design. This process has worked well for many decades. But if the owner decides to change the requirements, the impact on the project can be huge because all the work related to the original requirements must be redone.

By comparison, in the IT/software field, the process of gathering requirements is still relatively young and immature. The IT field generally does not take the disciplined approach to requirements that the construction industry typically follows. Without the requirements defined, traditional project management approaches are not as effective. The high **failure** rate of IT projects has been well documented (particularly by the Standish Group); much of that failure can be attributed to missing or poorly phrased requirements. As a solution, IT firms have developed project management approaches that work around the problem, such as agile approaches. In agile development approaches, the product is divided into smaller pieces of functionality and each piece is delivered via a smaller project. Instead of one long project, multiple short projects are undertaken to create the final product incrementally.

The IT field has made the problem worse by outsourcing development. If I'm doing the work in-house and I have a poorly stated requirement, I can just walk down the hallway to the person who gave me that requirement and talk it over until the requirement is clear. When the developers are 8,000 miles away, you can't do that. The output of many outsourcing software projects is very poor because the developers made guesses about what a requirement really meant (see **guessing**).

Poorly developed requirements are not always a deadly sin. In high-risk fields, such as pharmaceutical research or high-tech aerospace development, it is expected—and accepted—that the requirements will evolve as the project matures. When you're doing risky development, it is impossible to define all the requirements ahead of time.

A Case of Poor Requirements

In one IT project where I was the lead systems engineer, the project was turned over to someone with no experience in project management. The project manager took the entire IT staff to an off-site facility and just turned them loose. They spent a year working and at the end of it had no useable code, no documented requirements, and nothing to show for the $10 million they had spent. Moreover, the IT staff was demoralized and couldn't understand why they hadn't delivered a product.

The executives politely moved the project manager out of the way and hired someone with a strong project management background. Within a few months, we had a solid set of requirements that we were able to use to develop an industry-leading IT architecture.

Danger Signs

The first sign that poor requirements lurk is that there is no requirements document—approved and signed—before the actual work starts. That's a sure forewarning that the project will run into problems.

The next sign is if the project manager starts getting too many change requests that are related to missing requirements. If more than 10 percent of the change requests are against requirements, there's a danger that the product has not been thought through adequately.

Solutions

There is no shortcut to developing a product without understanding your requirements up front. The construction and the aerospace industries are the most mature in this regard. No construction work starts without having a thorough set of engineering drawings that show the requirements in great detail. In aerospace, it is the job of systems engineers to define the requirements for the final product.

The project manager needs to ensure that a sufficient amount of time is devoted to identifying requirements, analyzing them, and getting the customer to approve them. Without following this process, the team is likely to start working on the wrong product.

The old saying in project management "There's never time to do it right, there's always time to do it over" is especially true when it comes to developing your project's requirements.

Tips for Gathering Good Requirements

▶ *Ensure that sufficient project time and effort are devoted to gathering and analyzing the requirements.*

▶ *Begin product development once the requirements document is approved and signed.*

▶ *At the end of every phase of the project, validate the requirements to ensure that they were, in fact, the correct requirements and that nothing has changed on the customer side.*

60

Popularity

Popularity is the quality or state of being widely admired, accepted, or sought after. In projects, popularity becomes a "sin" when the project manager or team members are more concerned with being liked and accepted than with being effective and doing what's in the best interest of the project.

The Sin

Unfortunately, popularity is all too common in project environments. The need to be liked and accepted is a core human trait. However, some people aspire to be liked and popular more than others. Being a project manager is not an easy job and one of the most difficult aspects of leadership is making unpopular, but necessary, decisions.

Popularity usually manifests itself on projects when project managers face a tough interpersonal issue. For example, a project manager may choose to let a late project task languish instead of confronting the task owner head-on about the poor performance (see **lateness, laziness**). The project manager doesn't want to risk not being "liked" by the task owner.

A Case of Popularity

When teacher Christa McAuliffe was added to the flight crew of the space shuttle *Challenger* in 1986, the space mission became a national news story with a very high level of media attention. Despite repeated warnings from safety engineers, NASA chose to launch the *Challenger* on January 28, 1986. The shuttle was launched in temperatures below the safety threshold of the booster rocket O-ring ratings.

The decision to launch was primarily a popular decision born out of media attention; NASA sought to maintain the public's admiration and support. The decision resulted in an explosion that killed all seven members of the crew and led to hundreds of design and procedural changes that ended up costing several billion dollars. Additionally, the shuttle program subsequently became almost exclusively devoted to delivering defense and scientific payloads.

Danger Signs

Recognizing popularity can be very difficult, but the results are readily apparent. You must develop a strong sense of self-awareness to be able to identify those situations where you, as a project manager, are behaving in a popular way instead of the appropriate way.

One particular danger sign is "groupthink." If you seem to be relying on **consensus** to make tough decisions, you are probably behaving in a popular way and, more than likely, not making the best decisions.

Solutions

Take responsibility for the success of the project and run it like it's your own business—because it is. As a project manager, your team looks to you to provide leadership. Although you may not always be the most popular person on the team, your peers will eventually come to recognize that you are a strong, effective project manager.

Tips for Keeping Popularity from Harming Your Project

▶ *Accept that you will not always be liked.*

▶ *Understand that decisions are not always easy to make.* Rely on the advice of subject matter experts to guide your technical decisions at the project level.

▶ *Realize that you ultimately own the decisions you make.*

61

Powerlessness

Powerlessness is defined as lacking the authority or capacity to act (see **no authority**). In project management, the project manager and team may find themselves in a situation where they feel powerless to enable the project to proceed in a manner that will meet its objectives.

The Sin

Powerlessness results in a reduced capacity to act. A feeling of powerlessness often translates into failing to use available authority or influence effectively. The sin is allowing time to go by and things to happen without taking action.

Sometimes, project managers and team leaders can benefit from being provided alternatives that they may not have thought of. However, not all managers are willing to accept or act on views that are different from their own (see **not-invented-here**).

A Case of Powerlessness

In one project I was asked to support, the project manager and team had worked very hard for months to satisfy their customer.

Unfortunately, the harder they worked and the more overtime they contributed, the less control they felt they had over project deliverables, objectives, and results. Whatever they did, nothing seemed to have positive results. The situation finally "blew up" when the customer sensed that the project was out of control— the project team had lost credibility with the customer. The costs of this problem included removal of the project manager; reexamination of the goals, objectives, products, and capabilities of the project; a six-month unsuccessful effort to rescue the project; and loss of the contract.

An important lesson learned from this experience is the value of staying close to the customer and acting promptly on perceived problems.

Danger Signs

The danger signs of powerlessness include:

▶ Inability to achieve clarity or agreement on prioritized requirements (see **poor requirements**)

▶ Lack of clear leadership to move the project in intended directions

▶ Failure to make decisions in a timely manner

▶ Customer and stakeholder concerns that are not addressed proactively

▶ Ineffective communications that prevent the groups within a project team from having a common understanding (see **miscommunication**)

▶ Lack of information provided to the customer

- Absence of quality control activities (see **shoddy quality**)
- Continual changes in approach, reflecting the lack of steadfast purpose
- Too many uncoordinated initiatives that are not integrated and don't support one another
- Change for the sake of change
- Lack of a clearly defined project approach and methodology (see **poor planning**)
- Lots of activity but few results
- Surprises
- Inadequate skills and knowledge to accomplish the work
- Use of the wrong methods.

Solutions

The project manager must keep foremost in mind the customer's real needs and objectives—even when the customer needs help figuring out what these are! If the objectives of the project are not defined in a manner that meets the needs of all stakeholders, the first step is to gain agreement from the stakeholders on the deliverables and capabilities that will meet their real needs. An effective mechanism for accomplishing this is to ask the customer to host a "requirements workshop" attended by representatives of all key stakeholders. An experienced facilitator can help the participants define and agree on project goals and objectives. Time should be invested to determine the mission and scope of the project, and then to develop priorities so that the project effort can be phased to meet the most important needs first.

Another solution is to keep the customer and stakeholders involved during performance of the project. Hold regular meetings of representatives of the project team and the stakeholders to share information and to make sure the stakeholders buy into the work that is proceeding.

Still another solution is to request an external review. Often an objective evaluation will result in suggestions and ideas that can instill confidence and reinvigorate the project manager and team.

Providing training to improve skills, knowledge, and techniques may be useful. Training focused on improving teamwork can help overcome a feeling of powerlessness.

It's vital that the project manager take action quickly when she begins to feel a sense of powerlessness—the earlier such concerns are addressed, the better. Help can be provided by the project manager's manager, other project managers, resources such as process improvement or quality management staff that might be available within the organization, and even members of the project team.

Tips for Overcoming Powerlessness

▶ *Set realistic, clearly defined goals and objectives.*

▶ *Evolve the real requirements before undertaking project work.* Write a mission and scope document. Host requirements workshops. Establish priorities.

▶ *Maintain good communications with the customer and stakeholders* about what is really happening on the project.

▶ *Manage expectations to* that which is doable.

▶ *Provide leadership.* Involve the project team in major decisions, listen to advice, and take actions in a timely manner.

▶ *Ensure that the members of the project team are trained and experienced* in their disciplines.

▶ *Foster teamwork* and support of each other.

▶ *Don't lose sight of project objectives* in dealing with others and performing project work.

62

Prevarication

Prevarication means to speak falsely or misleadingly; to deliberately misstate or create an incorrect impression; to lie. Project managers who prevaricate will generate mistrust among project team members, which will inevitably have a negative effect on the team.

The Sin

Prevarication is lying. Regardless of whether the lie is flagrant or nuanced, the effect is the same. Lying destroys trust, and trust is perhaps the most important ingredient in any healthy relationship—personal or professional.

Lying has such a powerful effect on both the liar and his audience that even extraordinary accomplishments by extraordinary people can be diminished and entire careers damaged, destroyed, or summarized by a single lie. Richard Nixon's "I am not a crook" and Bill Clinton's "I did not have sexual relations with that woman" are two classic examples. If presidents can be defined by the lies they tell, so can project managers.

A Case of Prevarication

Alan was a newly hired project manager at Now Igotcha Consultants. Most of his team members initially considered him a well-meaning fellow, but they noticed that he was often involved in certain "misunderstandings."

An incident at work caused Alan's manager Bill to suspect that something was amiss. Alan's project team was expected to attend a nearby convention, but a huge winter storm was approaching. Bill and Alan decided at the last minute that instead of requiring the entire team to attend the convention, they would leave the decision up to each team member. They divided the list of team members to contact and agreed to make sure they heard from each person so no one would be left uninformed.

A few days later they heard from Brenda, who had attended the convention and was surprised to find that no one else from the project team was there. The storm had been much more severe than expected and she was upset that no one had told her attendance was voluntary. Alan, who was supposed to have called her, said that she should have known attendance was voluntary because he had left her a voice message. Brenda told Bill privately that she suspected Alan was lying: She hadn't received a voice message about the convention. Bill didn't know whom to believe, but the incident made him begin to worry about Alan and his project team.

Bill continued to hear troubling stories about Alan's prevarications from project team members, and it became apparent that Alan was losing the respect (see **disrespect**) of his team. Bill encouraged the team members to discuss their concerns with Alan directly, but they were unwilling to do so and he was obliged to honor their confidentiality.

After too many failed commitments, Bill met with Alan to discuss his history of bizarre behavior. Alan confessed that for years he had suffered from a crippling fear of failure and that he often protected himself by lying. He didn't like the person he had become and had recently begun seeing a therapist. Because Alan had lost the support of his team, Bill transferred him to another department and gave him one more chance.

Lies always have direct and collateral damage, no matter who you are or what the circumstances. We know the effects of lies don't stop with those directly involved. They extend beyond that person to another and another as the story is retold.

Tips for Dealing with Prevarication

▶ If you are like Alan, *try to figure out why you are lying.* Lying is often symptomatic of another problem, and you may continue to lie until you resolve that problem.

▶ If you are like Bill and one of your direct reports is lying, *nip it in the bud.* If you don't, you may appear tolerant of or even complicit in such behavior. If the liar has lost the support of the team, fire or move her so you can minimize the damage.

▶ If you are like one of the team members witnessing the lies, *speak up.* Don't make **excuses** for the behavior, tolerate it, or leave it unaddressed. Sometimes liars will stop lying to you if you call them on it. If enough people follow your lead, you may be doing yourself, the liar, and everyone else a favor.

63

Procrastination

Procrastination means deferring or delaying action needlessly, especially out of habitual carelessness or laziness. In project management, procrastination often results in missing a schedule target for a planned task, activity, or decision and can occur for several reasons, including carelessness, laziness, wishful thinking, fear, and risk management.

The Sin

Personal attributes such as **carelessness** or **laziness** may cause project managers to procrastinate and miss schedule targets for planned tasks, activities, or decisions, but project managers with these characteristics aren't likely to remain project managers for long. More often, procrastination occurs for other reasons—wishful thinking ("If I just wait a bit, things will improve"), fear ("If I act now, I may make a mistake"), or strategic risk management ("If I delay, the odds of success improve").

Communication **barriers** often obscure procrastination in project management. For example, when a project manager fails to hold a critical design review as scheduled, is the decision to delay a result of procrastination or is it a considered, deliberate, and informed decision? If the project manager does not communicate a clear rationale for the delay, stakeholders may assume he or she is procrastinating.

A Case of Procrastination

Procrastination rarely leads to positive project outcomes. A dramatic and fatal example of procrastination occurred during a World War II "project" made famous by the 1963 movie "The Great Escape," starring Steve McQueen. Author Mark Kozak-Holland writes about this project in his book, *Project Lessons from The Great Escape (Stalag Luft III)*.[1] Kozak-Holland describes the fateful night of March 24–25, 1944, when a series of significant setbacks (e.g., a frozen trap door, a tunnel that was too short, an air raid, cave-ins) foiled the plans of prisoners attempting to escape from a German POW camp. These setbacks delayed prisoners waiting to crawl through the tunnel to freedom—from the planned 60 escapees per hour to only 12 escapees per hour. In the end, only 3 men actually made it to freedom, 24 were captured and returned to prison camp, and 50 were captured and executed.

That night, project manager Roger Bushell procrastinated in several ways that led to the project's ultimate outcome. Why didn't he take action to minimize the impact of setbacks as they occurred? Was it because of **magical thinking**? Was he just waiting to see if things would improve? Why didn't he abort the escape when so many things went wrong? What happened to the stellar leadership skills he had demonstrated during the planning stages of the project?

---

1. Mark Kozak-Holland, *Project Lessons from The Great Escape (Stalag Luft III)* (Ontario: Multi-Media Publications, 2007).

While few of our projects risk the loss of life, procrastination can still have damaging consequences. Failing to execute a project as planned can lead to schedule slips, associated cost growth, and delays in the delivery of critical capabilities. Depending on our deliverables, procrastination can negatively affect other projects and programs, creating difficulties for the whole system, enterprise, or network.

Danger Signs

Although procrastination can occur at any time during the project lifecycle, its impact is perhaps most noticeable during implementation stages. Delays or mishaps during implementation have disastrous consequences throughout the remainder of the project, just as they did during the attempted prisoner escape. In projects with elaborate plans, schedules, and interdependencies, the impact of procrastination can ripple far beyond the immediate situation to affect all project deliverables and outcomes.

It can be difficult to recognize procrastination behind the assortment of communication barriers that plague projects (see **miscommunication**). Observing patterns over time, however, can help project managers and team members distinguish between random and isolated events that simply appear to be procrastination and events that truly demonstrate procrastination.

Screening for procrastination is rather simple and straightforward. One quick and almost foolproof test is to ask a suspected procrastinator to complete a reasonable task within a particular timeframe. The task can be as simple as placing a phone call to a third party on your behalf or providing you with some information that you know she already has. If the task is not done promptly, you have clear evidence of procrastination.

Solutions

The most effective way to avoid procrastination is to make as many decisions as possible early in the project lifecycle. This leaves little room for spontaneous decision-making or procrastination during project implementation, when the stakes are highest. Planning carefully can help project managers make decisions in advance. In addition to planning project tasks and activities, project managers can plan decisions, too.

For example, planning project reviews in advance can reduce decision-making burdens later. Thoroughly planned project reviews, also known as control gates, can follow a script written earlier in the project lifecycle. The script should include pre-established entry and exit criteria governing how the review will be conducted: If entry criteria are met, then the project team conducts the review according to plan. If exit criteria are met—i.e., if the review achieves its intended purpose—the project proceeds according to plan. If entry or exit criteria are not met, then the project should not proceed according to plan.

Writing data item descriptions (DIDs) is one way to capture entry and exit criteria for project reviews. Project teams can write DIDs (typically short, one-page documents) for each control-gate review or for each project deliverable. Measuring progress against the DIDs means simply comparing defined criteria against actual events, which reduces the opportunity for procrastination.

Tips for Overcoming Procrastination

▶ *Conduct a root cause analysis* to determine whether the cause of procrastination is a lack of information, a lack of good decision-making, conflicting or competing activities, fear, or a misunderstanding.

▶ *Take quick and effective steps to address the root cause* by supplying needed information, addressing important decisions, resolving priority conflicts, creating a positive work environment, or clarifying communications.

64

Promises

Promises are declarations assuring that one will or will not do something; vows. In project management, promises can be defined as the commitments established with, or accepted from, relevant stakeholders.

The Sin

In project management, one rarely hears anyone use the phrase, "I promise. . . ." Yet project managers and team members make commitments daily. Most projects exist in a context where they are surrounded by numerous other projects. Similarly, most projects operate under one or more levels of executive management. These factors directly contribute to project managers needing to establish and meet milestone dates, communicate these commitments, and report the project's status with regard to meeting the commitments.

Promises, or commitments, are essential for effective project planning, management, status reporting, and resource coordination. However, successful project managers are those who know which commitments they can accept and subsequently achieve, and which commitments they must either renegotiate or avoid entirely for reasons such as unrealistic objectives, significant constraints, or insurmountable obstacles (see **barriers**).

Generally, well-managed projects commence with the development of a plan, which is then maintained throughout the life of the project. This plan is not only an essential component on most projects, but it can be viewed as the primary artifact documenting the commitments made by the project manager, which will in turn affect the project team and other stakeholders. These commitments include milestone dates, intended system or product functionality, resource allocations, budgets, and risk mitigation activities. Hence, establishing achievable commitments and then tracking and ensuring their achievement are central to project success.

A Case of Promises

Unmet project commitments, or promises, are essentially the definition of project **failure**. In many industries, especially in the software and IT industries, overly ambitious projects that fail to meet cost commitments, schedule commitments, or feature commitments tend to be more common than projects that are completed on time, within budget, and with all required functionalities.

Even company executives can fall victim to their own unsubstantiated promises. For example, at one company where I worked as a software engineer, the executive team was responsible for long-range product feature planning and commitments. They also coordinated when we would demo new versions of our off-the-shelf software system at major conferences. The associated marketing and promotional campaigns often commenced six to nine months prior to the expected demonstration and release dates.

Although our software system was once the market leader in its category, the technical team never had the resources or time to add and debug all the promised features in any given release. Hence, as an organization, we chronically failed to get the released system to match all the claims being made by management and sales. As a consequence, although the system was more than adequate, and continued to evolve over time, any given release— when compared to the marketing and sales hype—consistently failed to come anywhere close to meeting buyers' expectations. Due to repeatedly failing to deliver the promised features by the promised dates, we slowly and steadily lost market share until, eventually, the company went out of business.

The myriad costs of failed promises and commitments are well known to most anyone involved with technology-intensive projects: excessive rework (see **excess**), deteriorating morale, long hours, in-fighting between teams (and team members), cost overruns, schedule overruns (see **lateness**), accelerated loss of senior or experienced talent, etc. Ultimately the largest cost is the loss of credibility of the person making promises that he fails to keep. After you earn a reputation as someone who makes promises you cannot keep, others will no longer trust you (see **prevarication**). Regardless of whether the others are executive management or the technical personnel on your own project team, once you lose their trust it is almost impossible to earn it back. Without trust, the likelihood of future success within that environment is vanishingly small.

Danger Signs

The earliest sign of someone who is prone to making promises he cannot deliver on can come in the interview stage—does his résumé appear to exceed his actual capabilities? This disconnect may not be easy to detect because some people not only write highly exaggerated résumés but also are good actors (i.e., smooth talkers) when being interviewed.

Promises, in particular those that cannot be met, are most costly and destructive when communicated at project inception or soon thereafter. Typically, a fair amount of optimism surrounds the start of most projects. Often, there is enthusiasm and even some level of excitement. What happens next, however, can lay the foundation for overall project failure. Specifically, program and project managers, and even technical personnel, often make somewhat vague references to being able to achieve particular milestone dates, certain levels of profit performance, etc. The people issuing such statements normally do not consider themselves to be making promises, but that's exactly what the people listening are hearing.

Hence, statements made in the early stages of a project that are interpreted by listeners as promises or other commitments are highly destructive to any subsequent efforts toward expectation management. And failure to meet the expectations of senior management, or of the customer or end-user organization, is essentially synonymous with project failure.

Solutions

Fortunately, there are a variety of solutions to the twin problems of promises that ultimately are not fulfilled and speculative statements that are interpreted as promises. One solution is to use highly incremental techniques and near-term milestones. This approach tends to reveal any disconnects between promises, expectations, and actual performance early in the project.

Another solution is to focus closely on recent data. IT and software projects are often subject to highly volatile circumstances, including changing tools, technologies, personnel, and requirements. In these situations, historical performance data tend to become irrelevant very quickly. Instead, recent data (ideally collected on a frequent basis) will tend to more accurately reveal the truth.

Third, an overall reliance on reasonable objective measurements, versus opinions about, for example, "percent complete," can help prove—or disprove—whether promises, requirements, commitments, expectations, etc., have any chance whatsoever of actually being met. This exact same data, when appropriately used, can help you ensure that the only promises you make will be promises that the facts indicate you can keep.

Tips for Keeping Promises from Derailing Your Project

▶ *Carefully monitor performance* to identify individuals who are prone to making promises or commitments they cannot meet.

▶ *Establish clear success criteria* for short-term goals to determine whether team members can make and keep reasonable commitments.

▶ *Collect and analyze recent performance data.*

▶ *Rely on objective measures* to determine if commitments are being met on the project.

65

Quitting

Quitting means stopping, ceasing, or discontinuing; giving up or resigning. In project management, quitting can mean settling for what is good enough or ignoring problems in an effort to finish the project as soon as possible.

The Sin

In the world of project management, quitting does not usually mean stopping work altogether—deciding that enough is enough and walking away from the project (although we all indulge in the idea occasionally). Rather, quitting in project management involves more subtle behaviors. The project manager who gradually drops her mission to create a high-quality product, for example, and settles instead for whatever is good enough is quitting in a sense (see **shoddy quality**). So is the project manager who, faced with ongoing **conflict** on the team, decides to just ignore it and puts his head down hoping that the project will quickly be over (see **hope**).

Giving up on quality often happens when the project manager faces significant organizational or resource hurdles (see **resource reallocation**); rather than continue to feel extremely frustrated, she decides to give in and settle for less. (This is not always a sin, however, because sometimes schedule and budget constraints make it necessary to settle for a lower quality product. In these situations, both the project manager and the customer should agree that a "good" product rather than an "excellent" product is acceptable.)

Ignoring conflict on a project is another form of quitting, one that is most prevalent when the interpersonal dynamics on a team are particularly challenging. An example is a cross-cultural, virtual team that is experiencing conflict but sees no easy path toward resolution. Another example is the project manager who, either because of personal style or lack of experience, shies away from being assertive and action-oriented in the face of conflict, perhaps in an attempt to be well-liked by team members (see **popularity**).

A Case of Quitting

In one case, a project manager quit on his team by failing to address conflict. The results were both tangible and significant. This project manager was the leader of a cross-cultural team operating virtually across many time zones. Team members came from many countries, some of which had long histories of armed conflict with one another. This demographic heightened risk factors on the project and was compounded by the fact that most of the virtual team members had never met one another.

However, the primary risk factor was the project manager himself, who put too much emphasis on team harmony and his personal likeability. This emphasis made the project manager come across as something of a cheerleader. He tried to be positive and encouraging, even in situations when he should have stepped in and actively worked to resolve chronic conflict. In essence, he was not assertive, he avoided addressing conflict, and he metaphorically put his head in the sand, hoping that the conflict would go away (see **magical thinking**).

Because the project manager was not assertive and did not work toward resolving conflict, he ultimately gave up on his team. As a result, team members became disillusioned and their motivation suffered. The team did not meet the project's original objective—to build an innovative software product required to solve a difficult service need. Instead, they delivered a somewhat mediocre solution that ultimately required substantial corrective work by another team. The project manager lost traction on his career path and the company faced retention problems as a number of the demotivated team members resigned.

Danger Signs

People often quit by having a passive response to conflict during the implementation and closing stages of a project, when the intensity is highest, people are fatigued, and significant levels of conflict have built up.

Project managers can recognize the signs within themselves and also external signals from team members. One internal signal comes from listening to "self-talk"—what are you saying to yourself? Are you saying, "Why should I keep trying? My team members can't get along with each other. Let's just finish this project as soon as possible."

An external sign of quitting is a project team that has been transformed by overt conflict into a sullen and quiet group of people (see **silence**). Another signal comes from team members who, when faced with an issue or problem, go directly to the project manager for support instead of working with another team member to resolve the problem. Project managers will usually find that their workload increases as intra-team interaction decreases.

Tips for Not Quitting

▶ *Act sooner rather than later when you perceive conflict on your team.* Rarely does conflict resolve itself over time, so waiting until the conflict has reached a high level is counterproductive. Instead, take a proactive approach and address conflict when it occurs.

▶ *Practice assertiveness skills.* A project manager can be both a "people person" and a good conflict-resolution agent. Take some chances during team meetings. Recognize that you do not always have to be liked by your team members. Ask others to help when possible.

▶ *Have a clear project charter* that addresses how conflicts will be resolved. Review the charter with the project team frequently.

66 Rebelliousness

Rebelliousness is defying or resisting established authority or tradition; the act of being insubordinate; the inclination to be defiant. Rebelliousness of team members often represents the greatest challenge for project managers who fail to appreciate the nature of their authority.

The Sin

Rebelliousness is a behavioral tendency that can exist in any professional setting and is often evident in project teams. To understand why, consider these two key aspects of projects: (1) Many organizations are structured in a matrix fashion, where project teams are made up of people across different work groups, and (2) the project manager traditionally represents an authority figure when it comes to leading projects.

In practice, these two project aspects are frequently in **conflict**. As project managers attempt to exercise their obligation (and perceived right!) to direct the efforts of the team, they quickly recognize that they have no real—that is, formal—authority to do so (see **no authority**). Since team members do not typically report to project managers administratively, they aren't inclined to follow anything resembling a "direct order," which is a basic tool of formal authority. The disconnect between the inherent need to tell people what to do and the formal authority to do so is one of the greatest challenges project managers face.

A Case of Rebelliousness

The company I was working for came to the realization that project management is a good thing and attempted to establish a project management structure. Unfortunately, company management was not as discriminating as they should have been regarding the project managers they formally anointed. Within this inaugural group was a very senior engineer who was accustomed to bossing people around. This approach had been successful for him in the past because he had been a formally recognized authority figure in the company's engineering department.

When he attempted to apply this style to his first job as a project manager in a cross-functional team environment, however, rebelliousness was rampant. The project team members simply did not accept his self-perceived authority. Therefore, although he was a knowledgeable and competent technical individual, he failed miserably as a project manager. His failure, of course, translated into project **failure**. In this case, rebelliousness resulted directly in wasted time, wasted money, and a substandard set of final deliverables (see **shoddy quality**). In addition, the ensuing state of perpetual conflict took a considerable human toll on many of the people involved in the project.

Danger Signs

We need only refer back to the definition of rebelliousness to understand its danger signs. Insubordination and defiance are key indicators of a bigger problem. These behaviors generally appear on a project for two reasons: (1) Team members disagree with either the direction the project manager is taking the project or a specific decision, and (2) team members simply do not want to follow the project manager's lead. The first reason is technically based and is relatively easy to spot; the second is interpersonally based and tends to be more confusing because it can take a variety of subtle forms. If you as project manager establish yourself as an authority figure, people will be much more inclined to want to follow you. But without formal authority, how do you proceed?

Solutions

For project managers, the key to reducing or eliminating rebelliousness begins with simply recognizing your lack of formal authority in the trenches—in other words, how the role plays out in real life. Many organizations tend to define the project manager's role as possessing considerably more authority than it does in practice. Project managers who don't recognize this gap between theory and practice are destined to lead a difficult existence.

The most successful project managers are those who are able to develop effective informal authority. Where informal authority is effectively established, rebelliousness is much less likely to be an issue.

The secret to cultivating effective informal authority is to truly understand the sources of power. The three types of power that correlate with authority are referent, expert, and informational; it's useful to possess all three.

Referent power is based in the ability to create a sense of loyalty by establishing strong interpersonal relationships. It requires charisma and other valued interpersonal skills. You can probably guess how much charisma the engineer in our case had.

Expert power stems from being recognized as extremely skilled or competent. People feel that they are likely to be successful if they are guided by your expertise. While this is a useful source of authority, it is usually not enough on its own.

Informational power derives from having superior knowledge of a situation. This leads directly to credibility. People will naturally be inclined to follow the person "in the know."

In popular lore, there are countless tales of how rebellion flourishes where authority is lacking. Project managers who recognize that formal authority is not a viable tool—and are able to replace that tool with effective forms of informal authority—are likely to be very, very successful.

Tips for Preventing Rebelliousness from Wreaking Havoc on Your Project

▶ *Know your limits.* It is important to understand the limits that have been placed on you. If you step into the project manager role believing you can simply tell people what to do, prepare for anarchy!

▶ *Establish a "presence."* Recognize that you'll need a substitute for lack of formal authority. The way you carry yourself says a lot. Demonstrate self-assurance. Behave as a commander would (short of issuing direct orders). Always stay calm and in control.

▶ *Feel the power.* Appreciate that you may be able to draw upon various sources of power to obtain compliance without conflict. Figure out whether referent power, expert power, or informational power is the right choice, given who you are and what you know. Then leverage that power in a way that discourages rebellion.

67

Resource Reallocation

Resource reallocation occurs when a source of supply, support, or aid, especially one that can be readily drawn upon when needed, is reassigned. In project management, resource reallocation becomes problematic when it has detrimental effects on the project or team members.

The Sin

Resource reallocation is a normal process in project management. It occurs within the project as well as between projects. As tasks and work packages are completed, personnel are routinely reassigned. In addition, personnel are reallocated to downstream tasks and to new tasks and work packages identified in the schedule.

Specifically, resource reallocation occurs in the following project situations:

▶ The effort in a work package is completed and the resources need to be reassigned.

- A specific resource is needed on another project at the same time to meet a schedule; the resources need to be reallocated or the schedule modified to eliminate the **conflict**.

- A higher priority project needs resources that are currently assigned to a lower priority project.

- Tasks on the critical path do not have the resources necessary for their timely completion, so resources are shifted to resolve the problem.

- It is not possible to hire or bring in resources from outside the company, so internal resources must be reassigned.

All these situations require that resources be reallocated to ensure that project goals are met. The normal process of resource reallocation becomes a project management sin when team members are not reassigned when work is completed, or when staff is not added to the project and assigned to planned tasks or work packages in a timely manner.

Often, a problem can be resolved by reallocating resources. However, much of the work that has already been completed may have to be reworked or reprogrammed and new objectives established.

A Case of Resource Reallocation

Most resource reallocation problems occur in response to outside forces. I was the deputy project manager of a major project involving a new high-speed railroad in the northeast corridor. The U.S. Secretary of Transportation had promised a powerful Massachusetts congressman that the new maintenance facility would be located in his state (see **promises**). This promise was made without any consultation with the project manager or me. The analysis performed on the project showed that the maintenance facility needed to be located in Delaware for three reasons:

1. The bulk of the traffic, by a ratio of approximately 10:1, was between New York City and Washington, D.C., not between New York City and Boston. Cars and engines operating south of New York City needing maintenance would have to deadhead to Massachusetts and return, which would be very expensive.

2. There was an existing facility in Delaware that only needed upgrading.

3. The increased cost was approximately $300 million and a two-year delay in the overall project schedule.

When the program manager and deputy program manager objected to the plan to locate the facility in Massachusetts, we were replaced. Resource reallocation operated at two levels in this case: one in facilities on the ground and the other in the organization chart.

The project was halted and a major reassessment was performed in accordance with the preferences of the new political team (see **politics**). The initial $1.75 billion project increased to $2.5 billion, with a two-year delay. In the end, the maintenance facility remained in Delaware because the increased cost was too much even for the new Secretary of Transportation to justify.

The biggest problem in making any resource reallocation work effectively on this project was the lack of communication between project management and the political stakeholders (see **miscommunication**). The two managers were focused on managing the project and solving internal problems and were relatively insensitive to changes occurring in the political landscape. Their successors, while less qualified as project managers, were much more attuned to the external environment and were able to bring the project to a successful completion. In this situation, resource reallocation became a political issue, external to the work of the project but significant in its impact.

Solutions

Training and experience can help project managers handle resource reallocation well, so that the process helps rather than harms the project. It is too easy and interesting to get involved in the project problems and ignore potential outside problems. This seems to be particularly true for engineers and less of a problem for MBAs!

Tips for Dealing with Resource Reallocation

▶ *Recognize that as projects proceed, it is normal to have to reallocate resources.*

▶ *Be aware and maintain communications with all stakeholders.* Projects are dynamic; it is not enough to focus just on time, quality, and cost or to meet specifications and budgets.

▶ *Make sure all the stakeholders are involved and understand the rationale* for resource changes. Do not rely entirely on the power of your position.

▶ *Maintain an environment of transparency* to achieve effective resource reallocation.

68

Rigidity

Rigidity is being stiff or unyielding, not pliant or flexible. In project management, rigidity can be defined as indifferently or defiantly clinging to policies, practices, and behaviors that are not well-suited to the unique characteristics of the project.

The Sin

Process is meant to provide a proven and predicable path to project success. This works perfectly if all of an organization's projects are similar. But it is a recipe for **failure** when an organization is working on complex projects. All projects must follow the same overall process to avoid **chaos**, but different projects require varying degrees of management control, documentation, lifecycles, and deliverables to avoid inappropriate rigidity.

What does rigidity look like?

▶ One-size-fits-all project processes

▶ Pressure to provide product solutions quickly

▶ Compulsory product lifecycle.

A Case of Rigidity

We were at a client site to determine whether to shut down a large, bleeding-edge technology project. We were told that the outsource partner was a disaster. Our implicit mission was to stop the hemorrhaging of money. The whispers and hints we heard were aimed at writing a recommendation to get rid of the vendor.

We interviewed the client and three groups in the client organization: the project managers with procurement authority, the technical project managers, and the users. We immediately identified conflicting direction from the client organization for:

▶ Formal, mandatory waterfall methodology procurement direction from the project manager that governed how the vendor would be paid

▶ Conflicting client direction from the technical project managers for agile development and testing methodology practices for integrating dozens of products

▶ No monthly reporting acknowledgments of this disconnect by the vendor or client.

What happened? The project manager with procurement authority didn't fully pay the vendor since work was not completed as contractually specified. That triggered the need for our assessment. The verdict: The rigidity of the procurement process was ignored by the client's technical project managers. Yet, the contractor, not the client, was **blamed**. Who was responsible for this rigidity? The client for setting up the vendor for failure or the vendor for agreeing to it? The client organization's structure allowed three different groups to provide direction to a vendor on a complex integration project. Next, the client management did not understand that the procurement contract was diametrically opposed to the development lifecycle. There was pressure to move quickly. Progress needed to be made fast, but management has responsibility for more than just funding. Management must discover and remove organizational obstacles such as rigid lifecycles before providing funding.

Danger Signs

Several organizational drivers tend to fossilize project practices:

▶ *Large organizations.* The corporate staff may mandate practices that work across functional lines. These rigid practices may suboptimize practices on a complex project.

▶ *Financial pressure.* When large organizations are not making money, all hands are on deck to get project work done and no resources are dedicated to removing rigid processes that are no longer aligned to organizational needs (see **misalignment**).

▶ *Low-growth organizations.* These organizations have limited ability to bring in new staff or new ideas, or to reengineer for success. They may rigidly stick to current project practices due to lack of time and manpower.

▶ *Heavy reliance on outsource partners.* Outsourcing may be legislatively mandated or it may be a cost-cutting reality. Organizations that outsource may lose the subject matter or domain experts who are the change catalysts or leaders. They have then lost the expertise needed to change, respond, and not get stuck in rigid project practices.

Solutions

Organizations must tailor project practices. Period. If there are not enough project resources, the organization has too many projects. Challenging times call for decisive action.

Tips for Loosening Up Rigidity on Your Project

▶ *Articulate when projects are going too fast* to appropriately balance cost, time, quality, and scope.

▶ *Take steps to ensure the organization does not fund projects without understanding how the scope is delivered.*

▶ *Identify **conflicts** in processes and lifecycles.*

▶ *Approach change in an incremental fashion,* focusing on one major change idea at a time.

69

Satisficing

Satisficing is a decision-making strategy that attempts to meet criteria for adequacy rather than to identify an optimal solution. In project management, satisficing is an intellectual or emotional choice to fall short of full business requirements or solution identification in response to time or team pressures when operating in an uncertain environment.

The Sin

Satisficing in project management relates to several key areas:

▶ *Time*

–Not accounting for newness

–Not allowing the time needed to interview all stakeholders to learn their requirements (see **poor requirements**)

–Not understanding the impacts of decisions or **assumptions**

–Not completing stakeholder analysis

–Inconsistently providing a work breakdown structure, schedule, budget, risk plan, and communication plan.

Project managers must be able to make recommendations on how much time is needed to accomplish the project's scope. If project completion dates are mandated, leadership must provide scope, quality, or cost decisions. It is leadership malpractice to provide goals without establishing a process that enables project success.

▶ *Scope*

–Not understanding the full scope and its product, project, and process impacts

–Not considering design alternatives

–Outsourcing requirements, project management, and system architecture decisions.

Project leadership cannot be outsourced. Staff augmentation is necessary and mandatory on large projects, but business domain decisions can't be delegated to outside the organization.

▶ *Budget*

–Not considering time or cost buffers for newness.

–Authorizing projects even if there is not sufficient funding.

A Case of Satisficing

I was hired by a client to rewrite a business requirements document (BRD) that a very competent project manager had begun. The original BRD was considered too ambitious, complex, and "techie." My task was clear: Simplify the requirements and gain agreement from 50 stakeholders in six weeks. This was aggressive but doable. The BRD was the lowest priority on a large customer sales order implementation—a mere speck on the organization's defined path to progress and success.

Project obstacles abounded (see **barriers**). Antagonistic project managers wanted to protect the success of their features by not providing technical exchange information; the outdated system was missing documentation, causing business rules to be ambiguous; the project management office was unstable due to reorganizations; there was organizational pressure to declare project success; and I was curtly reminded that my BRD was at the bottom of the organization's million-dollar pile of priorities.

I cut, slashed, and documented. I was required to change automated solutions to manual processes, as no one defended the value of automation efficiency. After I moved on to other consulting assignments, I heard that the BRD had been deleted, restored, removed, and then added back to the list.

Two years later, on a new engagement, I saw the effect of the cuts and the project office focus on budget rather than on an automated end-to-end process. As I was walking to the break room, I noticed the name of my BRD on a 30-foot white board. Twenty sales representatives were in the room, hunched over their laptop computers. They were being trained on manual sales reconciliation, which was now required because that capability had been removed from the requirements document. On the printer was a copy of the manual process necessary to book orders.

Two years earlier, the program office ignored the warnings I documented—they satisficed. After all, it was a low priority, or was it?

Danger Signs

This story demonstrates the adage that there is never enough time to do it right but there is always time to do it again—just maybe not with you at the helm.

Satisficing may lead to an inappropriately high estimation of one's skill to accomplish project work—when no risks occur! The other extreme is personal disillusionment when new technology fails, new stakeholders question your project planning assumptions, and risks rock your world and threaten project success. Why personal disillusionment? The project manager made a tacit or complicit choice to do only good-enough planning when management didn't provide enough time. The project manager then hoped (see **hope**) that the organization would not be looking for a political fall-guy (see **scapegoating**) when the planning was insufficient to uncover the needed requirements, dependencies, and organization-wide impacts.

Solutions

On small, low-risk projects, satisficing may well represent the best organizational use of resources. But it is a sin on all other projects. Project managers must tailor project deliverables to the level of newness involved in the project.

Tips for Avoiding Satisficing

▶ *Write business requirements* as if your boss will change.

▶ *Craft a business case* defining conflicts as well as benefits.

▶ *Create a project management plan* that is tailored to the level of newness involved in the project.

▶ *Plan for risks* as if the environment will change.

▶ *Build a communication plan* as if the stakeholders will change.

70
Scapegoating

Scapegoating is singling out one person to take the blame. When projects go awry, it can be common for participants to want to blame someone. The project manager is often the most obvious scapegoat.

The Sin

In project environments where communications are not effective and good team building is not in place, scapegoating can be common. It can manifest itself in several ways:

▶ Team members blaming each other for tasks not completed

▶ The project manager being blamed for any and all project problems

▶ The project manager placing the blame for problems on project stakeholders.

The context of the problem and how the scapegoating is handled really determine the extent to which projects are affected. Many project managers complain about not having complete authority to run their projects (see **no authority**). Then, when problems arise, they feel that blame is placed unfairly on them. A similar analogy is a sports coach who does not have the latitude to make all the decisions for a team but is fired when the team performs poorly. Scapegoating is often an emotional and symbolic reaction to show that change is being implemented to improve the situation.

Morale issues are always a cost of scapegoating. When one person is singled out for blame, a culture of fear is created, with project team members wondering who will be next. This can turn a productive team inefficient in a hurry (see **inefficiency**). Scapegoating can also be contagious. If team members see it being done, they may resort to it themselves.

Danger Signs

Look for unclear roles and responsibilities. As the project manager, if you don't have full authority to run your project, make sure you know who does.

Assess the culture. Interview stakeholders and other project managers about performance management on previous projects, how success is measured, and if the organization has a tendency to look for scapegoats.

One easy danger sign to notice is the number of parties involved in the project. If many parties are involved, there will be many lines of communication to manage—and lots of opportunity for **confusion**, which can result in scapegoating.

Scapegoating often arises during the closing stage of a project. Completing the project deliverables and getting customer acceptance are fraught with tension and emotion even in the best projects. With no time left to repair problems to achieve project success, stakeholders sometimes seek out scapegoats.

Solutions

When projects are managed in a matrixed organization, be it weak or strong, it can be easy to find scapegoats because roles and responsibilities are not necessarily defined or communicated well. To guard against this:

▶ *Assume you have total responsibility and act like it.* If you go into the project with that attitude, the tendency to scapegoat will be diminished. You probably have more control and authority than you think anyway.

▶ *Use tools like a responsibility assignment matrix to define and document responsibility early in the project.* If all team members understand what is expected of them, they will deliver; if they don't, they should know who to hold accountable.

▶ In projects involving contract resources for any role, *make sure that all roles and responsibilities are clearly spelled out and agreed to* in the contract.

The key is to understand the culture and clearly communicate roles and responsibilities. If you are talking about lack of authority early in the project, you are essentially stating a key project risk; do what you can to mitigate or avoid that risk.

Tips for Avoiding Scapegoating

▶ *Ensure that project communications are clear and steady.*

▶ *Keep the top three issues and risks on your regular status reports.* Make sure that every opportunity is given to address these before they become showstoppers.

▶ *Involve your stakeholders and team members* in preventing problems. This will create a cohesive team approach and allow less of a chance to target individuals to blame.

71

Shoddy Quality

Shoddy quality refers to an item produced in an inferior way, with inferior ingredients or inferior workmanship. For project management, the definition can encompass less tangible aspects, like process quality.

Project management is a process, and its outputs or products are the plans, controls, and lessons learned from the execution of a project. While the quality of project management may not correlate directly to the quality of the output of the project, a shoddy-quality project management process will likely result in a poor-quality output. Not only will the deliverables suffer, but the project will likely experience cost and schedule problems as well.

The Sin

Shoddy quality is common in project management. If "what you measure is what you get," failing to measure something usually means you won't get much of it. We can define quality as "fit for use." How fit for use is the project management process? The scope of a process is an important aspect. When does the project management process start? Too often the process is weak or lacks the ability to decline a project or to halt or redefine it significantly after it has started.

Project management has a design range under which it operates best (just as homes have a design temperature and engines have an operating range). If a project gets too far out of the project management process operating range, say way ahead or behind schedule, over/under budget, or with deliverables that have significant quality problems, a poor-quality process will react in ways that introduce **inefficiencies** and waste. To avoid shoddy quality, the project plans and parameters may need to be reset to bring the project management process back into its operating range.

Another viable definition of quality is conformance to standards. Many tend to think of guidelines or norms like those defined in common public methodologies or bodies of knowledge as standards, while they are really just a good basis for standards. Every organization that carries out projects needs an objective means of evaluating its processes and their performance. This is essential to assessing and improving project management quality, particularly to identifying and correcting shoddy quality.

A Case of Shoddy Quality

One project **failure** that can be attributed to the shoddy quality of project management is the NASA *Challenger* tragedy.

Technical and design problems are inherent with the project challenge. The inability of those with the knowledge and concerns about the problems to communicate with the managers of the project, who can effectively address those concerns, reflects an abject failure of the process (see **miscommunication**). The process used in the NASA *Challenger* project was not "fit for use" where it was applied. If it were, there might still have been a tragedy, but the project management process would not have been the assignable cause.

Communication is a key element of project management process quality. The concerns of well-qualified engineers and technicians regarding component problems were not communicated in a way or in a context that the problems were understood or addressed in a manner consistent with their severity. The adage about the sweetness of met budget and/or schedule being short-lived when taken with the bitterness (and too often tragedy) of shoddy quality is as true for products or the result of projects as it is for the project management process.

Danger Signs

The key to recognizing quality problems is having (1) a definition of what a problem is and (2) a way to measure the conditions within that definition. Measures do not have to be quantitative; they can be as subjective as "I know it when I see it, and that's not it."

Process, process measurement, and quality definitions are essential. A good rule of thumb is that the cost of correcting a problem goes up by a factor of 10 for each phase that the problem "escapes." So if you have a four-phase process, a problem introduced in the first phase will cost 1,000 times more to fix after delivery to the customer than it would if it were discovered and fixed in the first project phase.

Solutions

Despite our best possible efforts, things can and do go wrong. Of course, our efforts are not always the best possible. By recognizing that everything (at least in business) is a process and by insisting on the highest quality and on continuous improvement, we can avoid or mitigate the consequences of shoddy quality.

The best way to avoid shoddy project management quality is to distinguish between the quality of the process and the quality of the projects to which it is applied. The quality movement of the 1970s and 1980s espoused the notion that the primary cause of quality problems is the failure to distinguish between common causes of variation and special causes of variation. Process flaw problems stem from common causes, and project and project team problems are common symptoms of those problems. Addressing the symptoms, even if done well, will only postpone disaster. Project or project team problems are special causes and must be fixed or mitigated as they occur.

Tips for Keeping Shoddy Quality from Dragging Your Project Down

▶ *Define the scope of the process* so that the project doesn't get out of the project management process operating range.

▶ *Establish an objective means of evaluating* an organization's project management process.

▶ *Decide on the measurements of success* at the outset.

72

Shortsightedness

Shortsightedness is generally defined as nearsighted, lacking in foresight. In project management, shortsightedness can blur long-term thinking and thus hamper a project's ultimate success.

The Sin

Shortsightedness is not so much a sin, but more of a limitation. It refers to the ability to see and focus clearly on things that are close up, while being less able to discern things that are farther away. Shortsightedness becomes a sin when you know you have it but you fail (or refuse) to take any corrective action.

In many ways, shortsightedness can be a good thing, especially in complex undertakings such as projects. We have to be aware of a lot of details, able to understand what is currently happening on the project, and focused on immediate issues such as cost control, resource allocation, task completion, progress monitoring, team motivation, and stakeholder satisfaction.

The problem arises when we are so focused on the here-and-now that we fail to look ahead and see what is coming. In particular, some future issues may require us to take action now. It is also vitally important to maintain a clear vision of the final objective and goal of the project, the end point toward which we are striving. We need to make short-term decisions in light of the longer term, and that requires a degree of longsightedness.

Danger Signs

Failure to keep a long-term perspective can result in suboptimal management of the project, as we react to the immediate circumstances in a way that prejudices overall project success. For example, a client may demand inclusion of an additional feature in our project that is currently out of scope (see **creep**) but that we could fit in by rearranging the schedule and reallocating resources. While taking these actions might keep the client happy in the short term, if the change results in overall delay to the project or the inability to deliver a coherent solution, we might find we have solved an immediate problem but created a bigger one.

Another example of shortsightedness is "rolling-wave planning," which is often cited as a sound project management practice. Rolling-wave planning encourages a focus on the short term in a long-duration project, planning the next period in considerable detail but developing only an outline plan for the remainder of the project. While this approach offers the benefit of ensuring close control over the immediate future, it increases the danger of losing sight of the longer term.

A Case of Shortsightedness

The problems that occurred when the new £4.3 billion Terminal 5 opened at London's Heathrow Airport in March 2008 were caused largely by shortsightedness. There was **chaos** on the terminal's opening day, with scores of flights canceled and thousands of bags lost, resulting in what the British government called "national humiliation." This high-profile, complex project failed for several reasons, but it has emerged that one consequence of the strong focus on meeting the publicly advertised opening date was a decision to cut the time allowed for staff training. British Airways Chief Executive Willie Walsh told a British government inquiry in May 2008 that "The training regime was compromised because of delays in completing the building." As a result, baggage handlers had problems with the state-of-the-art new baggage system, check-in staff were unable to log in to their consoles, and security staff didn't know where to park their cars.

Solutions

Shortsightedness in projects can be overcome in two main ways. First, it is essential for the project manager and the project team to keep a long-term perspective at all times, even when considering immediate issues. All project decisions must be made in light of the overall project objectives, asking whether this decision moves us toward or away from our goal.

Second, the project manager and team need a way of looking ahead into the future, scanning the horizon to identify what is coming and making proactive plans to respond in a timely manner. Sometimes this means acting in advance to prevent unwelcome events or circumstances, or to position the project to take advantage of potential upsides. This is the realm of risk management, which acts as a forward-looking radar for the project.

Even when the future is uncertain or ambiguous, the risk process can identify major threats and opportunities, and the project can be steered accordingly. Potential future events that could affect the project can be identified using creative risk identification techniques such as brainstorming and workshops, analytical approaches like assumptions analysis and root cause analysis, and reviews of historical project data such as checklists and post-project review reports. Other, broader techniques can also be used to visualize the future, such as scenario analysis, appreciative inquiry, futures thinking, and **gaming**.

The answer for physical shortsightedness is usually to wear some kind of spectacles, and these can take three possible forms. Sometimes glasses are prescribed specifically for use when looking long distances. An alternative is bifocals, which strengthen the ability to see both close up and farther away. The third option is vari-focal lenses, which are infinitely variable and allow the wearer to adjust his vision depending on where he needs to focus.

In the same way, if our ability to understand and manage our projects in the short term is effective, we may need simply to supplement this with an effective risk process that provides us with a view farther out into the future. If, however, our project control is generally weak, it might be better to adopt a bifocal approach, which will give us both close-up and far-off information. Best of all is a flexible method that can help us change our depth of focus as required, seeing the immediate, the mid-term, and the distant with equal clarity. A properly executed risk management process can meet these needs and is an effective way to deal with the problems arising from shortsightedness.

Tips for Overcoming Shortsightedness

▶ *Ensure that the project team is constantly focused on the ultimate objectives of the project* and that team members clearly understand the reason for the project and what it must deliver.

▶ *Assess all near-term project decisions* in terms of whether they move the project toward the goal or away from it.

▶ *Use the risk management process as a forward-looking radar* to scan the future for potential events and respond proactively.

73

Silence

Silence is the absence of sound or conversation. Whether it is intentional or accidental, silence is anathema to successful project management.

The Sin

"Silence is golden"? For project managers, "Silence is leaden." The projects we're working on are often all about sharing information or facilitating communication; it's ironic that the sin of silence visits itself on these projects so often.

Many of the people we work with on projects are technical and are highly skilled in their field of expertise; by their very nature they may be less than communicative. Although they may be more comfortable in a silent or uncommunicative mode, that just doesn't work for a project: Managing a project in silence is like trying to build a 50-story tower with hand tools.

A Case of Silence

I was planning for a large-scale seismic project in Northern Alberta that involved over a dozen distinct stakeholder communities. One of our first and most important project tasks was to identify each stakeholder, and more specifically, determine what each stakeholder expected from the project. It would have been easy for us to assume (see **assuming**) that this project made sense for all the players, since it promised (see **promises**) benefits for all.

Fortunately, we didn't make that assumption; instead, we made a point of having someone on the project team talk to every stakeholder and draw them out on what they were expecting. Beyond improving our understanding of the project stakeholder community, this approach forced all the team members to exercise their stakeholder communication "muscles." Most of them had never been asked to directly engage with a project stakeholder community before.

Good thing we did. We found out that the chief of the First Nations reserve close to where we would be surveying expected our project to employ young men from his reserve in cutting bush and removing slash to make way for the seismic lines. This seemed to be a reasonable expectation.

When we conferred with the provincial environmental agency, however, they indicated that they considered the area we'd be working in to be "environmentally sensitive." They expressed a strong desire—close to a direct order—that we minimize or eliminate cutting bush entirely and instead helicopter in and out everything we could for the project.

If we had simply assumed alignment ("This project is good for everybody involved, isn't it?"), these two reasonable but opposing expectations (see **misalignment**) would have at the very least slowed things down and possibly caused us to lose our winter work season; at worst we would have upset the chief and his people and possibly faced a blockade.

In this case, numerous conversations took place. We actively involved the executive sponsor in helping resolve the situation, we engaged the entire project team in discussing options and alternatives, and we made efforts to ensure that the full stakeholder community participated in reviewing the alternatives. In the end, a compromise was reached: limited cutting, with training for all participants (including members of the First Nation) in minimal-impact brush clearing.

Without open and active discussion among all the players, this situation could have snowballed into a project killer.

Danger Signs

Unless you're working on a classified military project, be wary of those who would communicate on a need-to-know basis (see **miscommunication**). "Need to know" too often means you're dealing with someone who likes the idea of having information that others don't. Maybe it makes them feel powerful (see **ego**); maybe they believe it justifies their position.

It's a bad idea and a bad approach in any case. Deciding not to make all project information available to the entire project team and the stakeholder community may cause you to miss something important—a question that someone doesn't get a chance to ask, a connection between two important elements that isn't seen, a risk that gets missed entirely until it becomes a project issue. (The only reasonable exception, of course, involves personal and personnel issues.)

By declaring a need-to-know basis for a project, you're telling the team that you will be intentionally keeping information from them, or that you'll decide what they should and shouldn't see or know, clearly implying that you know better. This attitude not only impacts project team morale, but also disengages important team players and may endanger the success of the project overall. How successful can a project be if members of the team feel like second-class citizens?

When only "core" team members are invited to project meetings, a red flag goes up. It's a good idea for people to make the best use of the time they have available on a project, but let them choose not to attend meetings where they're not adding value or getting information they need rather than telling them they can't attend.

The project sponsor should set the communications tone and should be the first enemy of silence on the project. "Sponsor" is an active verb, not just a noun, and the sponsor should be expected to model open communication with the team and stakeholder community—and to actively discourage silence.

You can tell when silence has caused a problem on a project: Something blows up (and something *will* blow up if people aren't talking to each other) and people start asking questions like "Did anyone know about this before?" or protesting, "No one told me."

A culture of silence can be attacked early in a project and an open communication discipline can be put in place—modeled by the project manager and the sponsor. Once a culture of silence settles in, the damage is much harder to repair.

Tips for Counteracting Silence

▶ *Conduct risk assessment.* Silence poses a risk to the project in that the right information isn't shared with the right people at the right time. Make a plan to deliberately not be silent.

▶ *Identify and communicate with stakeholders.* Each stakeholder—anyone who can impact or be affected by the project—should be clearly identified, along with what they expect from the project and what deliverables the project needs to plan to meet those expectations. Getting a clear understanding of stakeholder expectations is a good first step in launching a comprehensive, silence-killing communications plan.

74

Surrender

To **surrender** is to give up, to yield to the power
of another, or to relinquish possession of something
that has been granted. In project management,
this can mean giving up on a project goal, sacrificing
one of the constraints, or yielding on a demand
for needed resources. In each case, it means not
completing the project as well, as soon, or for as
little money as it should have been.

The Sin

Giving up on a project overall is the most extreme instance of surrender. The sin can occur in lesser degrees throughout the life of the project, however.

Surrendering on the project constraints of cost, time, or resources means not fighting for what you know the project needs. Surrender is when the project manager doesn't fight hard enough or just gives in. The project manager has to put up a good fight and not relinquish responsibility for making a strong case for what the project needs.

Sometimes surrender takes the form of a person assuming an accommodating style of handling **conflict**. That is, the person yields to the other party's way, even if doing so is not in the best interest of the project. Giving in is often the easy way out of an uncomfortable situation.

Another problem related to surrender can arise when the project manager is intimidated by senior staff. It's unlikely a project will get the needed resources if the project manager is hesitant in approaching senior staff. The project manager has to champion the project's cause.

Surrendering on a constraint or issue is appropriate at times. For example, if a person realizes she is wrong, surrendering on that point is the right thing to do. On occasion, surrendering on a point about which another member of the team feels strongly will allow you to get a concession in return.

A Case of Surrender

In the book *Outliers: The Story of Success*,[2] author Malcolm Gladwell relates the story of an airliner that crashed coming into a New York airport. One factor that contributed to the crash was the interaction between the plane's flight engineer and the air traffic controllers. When the conversation was later reviewed, it was determined that although the language the engineer used was appropriate in a crisis, it was overly deferential to the air traffic controllers. In response to the air traffic controllers acting "pushy," the flight engineer effectively surrendered his authority by not forcefully demanding the action needed.

---

2. Malcolm Gladwell, *Outliers: The Story of Success* (Boston: Little, Brown and Company, 2008).

Danger Signs

One way to screen for this sin is to determine whether team members are unwilling to sign a project charter. If they are not, that is a strong indicator that they are not really committed to the project and may be willing to surrender at the first sign of difficulty.

A consultant I know was reviewing a large project that failed. It had been well funded and the sponsor was a very powerful politician who had brought together all the resources needed. This sponsor also gave the project high priority. Yet the project failed. When the consultant reviewed the specifics, he found that no members of the team had signed the charter. When he asked them why they wouldn't make the formal commitment, he got answers like, "We don't sign internal documents." Apparently, they didn't want to be held accountable. If you believe you are accountable, you are less likely to surrender.

Solutions

Every project inevitably runs into difficulties, but the project manager and team do not have to surrender to these difficulties. The atmosphere created for the project can effectively eliminate the option of surrender. By communicating and demonstrating a strong belief in the project's goals, a project manager can create energy, enthusiasm, and determination in the project team and the key stakeholders—and leave no room for anyone to surrender to challenges that arise.

Creating the expectation that problems will be solved also works against the inclination to give in.

Tips for Avoiding Surrender

▶ *Get a formal commitment* from everyone involved.

▶ *Clearly communicate to senior staff the resources that are needed* for the project.

▶ *Ensure that the dynamics within the team are conducive to problem-solving.*

▶ *Create an atmosphere where surrender to challenges or difficulties is not an option.*

75

Suspicion

Suspicion is the state of mind or feeling of someone who suspects something, especially something wrong, on little evidence or without proof. Many actions on a project require some degree of trust or confidence in teammates. Suspicion undermines the trust and cooperation necessary to develop an effective team and can spread like a cancer.

The Sin

The potential for a suspicious environment exists wherever individuals work together. Suspicion is a personal trait that relates to feelings of security. An environment of uncertainty will give rise to suspicion.

When suspicion occurs in project management, it can be very counterproductive. Suspicion manifests itself when members of the team or the project manager are perceived to have agendas that differ from the goals of the project. When team members lose their trust in a person or in a plan, their productivity suffers.

Suspicion can arise in many aspects of the relationship between the project manager and members of the team. Why is team member x invited to a meeting but not team member y? Is another team member being favored? What are they really talking about in the project manager's office?

A Case of Suspicion

Our project was proceeding relatively on time and within budget when the vice president of our division called a meeting—in fact, he stood up on one of the desks at the end of the room where we were working and announced that the rumors of our division being spun off were not true. Up until that time, we were only peripherally concerned since the rumors seemed outlandish. Our suspicions were aroused by his actions and were reinforced when he resigned the following week. The level of suspicion increased significantly and the team's productivity dropped proportionally as increasing numbers of people got involved in discussing our suspicions that the rumors were true.

Danger Signs

Suspicion often takes the form of rumors that are upsetting to the normal productivity of team members. The damage that suspicion causes is a function of the impact of the rumors and the degree of upset they cause.

When project team members are distracted from their project goals by discussing suspicions and rumors, productivity suffers. Depending on the specific incident that raises suspicions, morale and turnover can be adversely affected. For example, suspicions of a staff reduction can cause individuals to look for other positions as a defensive move.

Solutions

Francis Bacon said: "There is nothing makes a man suspect much, more than to know little, and therefore men should remedy suspicion by procuring to know more, and not keep their suspicions in smother."

There is no real solution to the sin of suspicion other than for a project manager to be open and aboveboard in all actions so that the project team develops a strong sense of trust. Unfounded and negative suspicions either will not arise or will be quickly dismissed.

Tips for Conquering Suspicion

▶ *Keep the project team aware of actions that might impact them personally.*

▶ *Promote transparency in decision-making.*

76

Tunnel Vision

Tunnel vision is a drastically narrowed field of vision; an extremely narrow or prejudiced outlook; narrow-mindedness. In project management, tunnel vision is the rigid attachment to a single goal or very limited set of goals at the expense of everything else.

The Sin

Anyone in project management can fall prey to tunnel vision, causing them to lose the big-picture view. Perhaps the most glaring enabler of tunnel vision in project management is the belief that adhering to the originally defined scope, budget, and schedule is what defines success. This ill-conceived notion is captured in the familiar adage, "plan the work, work the plan." That simplistic statement has led many inexperienced project managers to assume that once a robust plan is in place and serves as a single goal, all that remains is to faithfully and rigidly execute the plan.

In a world that's constantly changing, a "stay the course" tunnel vision mentality that blocks off input and learning (see **barriers**) can be very dangerous in any field or walk of life. Tunnel vision is all too common in project management, closing off the learning and adaptation that are crucial to keep projects on course, especially in changing circumstances.

On a project, one manifestation of tunnel vision is meeting traditional project success goals like "on time" and "within budget" but ending up with unhappy customers. Another common example is when traditional status reporting is not working— project status reports spike from green to red immediately, without any warning.

A Case of Tunnel Vision

At a client organization, a project manager was heard declaring, "Over my dead body will we change anything on this project plan." This person insisted on blocking the regular adjustments necessary to keep abreast of changes in business conditions, requirements, and project context. As a consequence, while the project did not fail outright, the business customers were unhappy with the delivered functionality. The project manager thought the team delivered what was asked for, but it surely wasn't what the customers needed and it came too late to be of any value.

The direct cost in this case was the diminished business value associated with a product that didn't meet business needs. Indirect costs ranged from a damaged relationship between the business and delivery organizations to hostility between the project manager and management. Morale suffered all around, too.

Tunnel vision usually has the effect of taking a project either completely off a cliff into **failure** or bringing it dangerously close to the precipice.

Danger Signs

Locking down artifacts early and subjecting them to rigid change control is a serious warning sign of tunnel vision. When teams start to lock in anything—plans, requirements, or other artifacts—and use phrases like, "I know our customer is requesting this, but the <insert artifact here> says . . . ," it's clear evidence of the problem.

Solutions

The best way to guard against tunnel vision is to institutionalize learning. For example, with agile methods, learning is accomplished early and often through project retrospectives. After every one-to-three week iteration, teams take a step back and collectively reflect on what is working well and what needs improvement. All members of the project team have input into the discussion of the status quo and any required improvements.

Another great anti-tunnel vision practice from agile methods is the iteration review meeting. This is where the team presents its project results—typically a product increment, developed in the past one- to three-week iteration—to its business customer and any other project stakeholders. Business customers and other project stakeholders then provide valuable feedback on the results. This feedback is used for product improvement and project steering.

Tips for Overcoming Tunnel Vision

▶ *Always stay open to learning.*

▶ *Find structured ways* (like iterative project retrospectives and incremental product reviews) *to institutionalize learning.*

▶ *Get accustomed to and comfortable with accommodating the changes* that come with learning.

▶ *Realize that overcoming tunnel vision involves more of a shift in attitude and behavior* than a change in tools and techniques.

77

Whining

Whining can be defined as complaining in a peevish, self-pitying way. It is easy to decide to complain, or to whine, rather than to do. Many people prefer to point the finger at others and not participate in efforts to effect change. This means that they are comfortable with the status quo even though they claim that "nothing ever changes here."

The Sin

A key concept in project management is the usefulness of lessons learned. *A Guide to the Project Management Body of Knowledge (PMBOK® Guide)* notes this importance, recognizing that the *PMBOK® Guide* itself is continually evolving and includes both traditional and emerging project management practices. Each project is an opportunity for learning.

As project professionals, we need to use historical information, expert judgment, and lessons learned as appropriate, but we also must recognize that we have the opportunity to effect and embrace change. We no longer work in an environment where business as usual is good enough. Our world is constantly changing, especially since we are doing so much work globally and are relying so often on virtual teams that may never meet face to face on a project. Our projects and programs also are becoming extremely complex. This means we cannot continue to do work in the same way that we did it 20 years ago, 10 years ago, or even last year. While some of the processes we followed in the past are still applicable, we need to constantly look for alternatives that improve effectiveness, time to market, and our ability to meet the expectations of our customers.

Whining is counterproductive in this environment. It is incumbent on each of us to take the initiative to change what needs to be changed in our work on projects and to continue to use those practices that have served us well in the past. Now is the time to actively focus on continuous improvement. As the former, successful basketball coach at UCLA, John Wooden, said, "It's what you learn after you know it all that counts."

If we whine on our projects, our negative attitude can affect others, demoralizing and demotivating our team members. If we adopt a whining attitude rather than a winning attitude, we will approach each day assuming that nothing can possibly go right, that the problems of the past will remain. With this attitude, our projects likely will not be delivered on time, will be over budget, and will fail to meet our customers' expectations. Even early successes that we could build upon will be forgotten as whining detracts from every accomplishment.

Typically, we **blame** the level we do not see. For example, we tend not to blame our immediate project manager if we are team members or our project sponsor if we are the project manager because we interact with these people on a regular basis. Instead, we blame the next higher or lower level that we rarely interact with during the project. As a result, we feel **powerless** to effect change. We adopt an attitude of hopelessness rather than working to convince people of the importance of project management or meeting with reluctant team members to show to them the benefit of the project to the overall strategies of the organization.

This approach is common on many projects. We realize that the best approach to solving problems and resolving conflicts is to use collaboration or confrontation, but instead we use **avoidance** as our preferred approach and do not take responsibility for change. As a result, the project that might really make a difference to our organization may never even be proposed.

This whining attitude causes the organization as a whole to suffer. Negative publicity can result, and a project may go on indefinitely. Resources may be underutilized and the organization's strategic goals and objectives may never be met.

In today's environment, we simply cannot whine; we must instead *do*—and ensure that we put our best efforts into our work. Only then will our projects truly contribute to organizational success.

A Case of Whining

Recently, I had the opportunity to conduct a project management maturity assessment. Although the assessment had the support of the executive team, a whining attitude prevailed at all levels throughout the organization and was evident in most of the interviews I conducted. This organization was very successful but now was entering a new area. A number of people who had recently been hired to support the new program felt powerless. They believed the company's insistence on using practices and procedures it had used for the past 50 years was negatively affecting the new project.

Many of the findings in the assessment report reflected this whining attitude. When the report was presented to the executive team, they were surprised at the number of problems noted and the number of recommendations suggested to improve the state of the overall project management practice. Nevertheless, they failed to share the report with the people who participated in the process, even though it had been promised to them, and did not act on any of its recommendations. Unfortunately, the whining attitude continues in this company, damaging morale and limiting success.

Danger Signs

As project managers we need to be alert to whining and to confront and resolve its underlying problems as soon as possible. For example, if we note that a team member is argumentative, is negative in meetings, does not speak up, transfers responsibilities to others, or even sets extremely high standards that are impossible to meet, we need to recognize that this person may be a whiner and that his negative attitude can affect the entire team. As the project or program manager, we need to meet with this person and ask him about any problems being experienced or ideas that could help the project. We need to demonstrate a proactive attitude and to work to convince whiners that they are essential to the success of the project—and that they must contribute fully.

On a personal level, we cannot assume that we are powerless even in large organizations. We are the people who are actively practicing project management, so we need to take our ideas and sell them to others. Even if some of our ideas are not adopted, we need to continue to make the business case for something we feel can help our project, or our organization, in its quest for success.

Tips for Overcoming Whining

▸ *Have the team prepare a charter that sets forth its operating procedures and shows the members' commitment to one another.* This charter can state actions the team can take on its own without involving the project manager and can also describe a process to follow if something needs to be escalated to the project manager or even to the next level.

▸ *Focus on team-based rewards and recognition systems rather than solely emphasizing individual accomplishments.* Such a team-based approach can help foster project commitment, especially if team members participate in its development.

Assessment Tool
Which Sins Are Plaguing Your Project?

Think about your current project. From the list of 77 deadly sins, circle 7–10 that are most evident or are causing the biggest headaches on your project.

Acquiescence Assuming Avoidance Barriers
Blaming Blinders Bureaucracy Carelessness
Chaos Charity Close-mindedness Cluelessness
Complacency Conflicts Confusion Consensus
Copying Cowardice Creep Democracy Despair
Deviation Dispassion Disrespect Dysfunction
Ego Excess Exclusion Excuses Failure
Favoritism Fragmentation Gaming Guessing
Haphazardness Helplessness Hope Immaturity
Inattentiveness Indecision Inefficiency
Inflexibility Isolation Lateness Laziness
Magical Thinking Malfeasance Meetingitis
Misalignment Miscommunication Mismanagement
No authority Not-invented-here Obtuseness
Omission Opposition Politics Popularity
Poor Planning Poor Requirements Powerlessness
Prevarication Procrastination Promises Quitting
Rebelliousness Resource Reallocation Rigidity
Satisficing Scapegoating Shoddy Quality
Shortsightedness Silence Surrender Suspicion
Tunnel Vision Whining

How are the sins you circled related?

Which aspect of your project is experiencing the most difficulty in these areas?

Are you personally guilty of more than a few of these sins?

Awareness is the first step. Once you understand and can articulate your most challenging people issues on a project, you can begin to formulate approaches to resolving them. Perhaps the case studies in each chapter will give you some ideas about how to start addressing the particular sins that are keeping your project from achieving key milestones and ultimately successful completion.

Adapted from *Anytime Coaching: Unleashing Employee Performance* by Teresa Wedding Kloster and Wendy Sherwin Swire. © 2009 by Management Concepts, Inc. All rights reserved.

Assessment Tool
What Are the Challenges on Your Project?

Write down the situations you find most challenging, stressful, or difficult in working with people on your projects. As you reflect on your discomfort, consider what these areas could be signaling about how you approach issues. What is another way to look at the difficulty you are experiencing? Have you intentionally or unintentionally played a role in creating the difficulty? What might your team members' perspectives be?

For example, your need to achieve consensus among your team members for every decision might be weighing your project down. Can you exercise leadership without creating a sense of powerlessness and complacency on your project? Do you view acquiescence or opposition by your team members as negatives—or as opportunities that you can make work to the project's advantage?

The examples below present hypothetical issues and relate them to several of the 77 deadly sins. List other issues you are experiencing on your project, relate them to the sins, assess your role and approach, and then develop (or refer back to) some tips that can help you deal productively with each issue. The key is to be able to view the issue through your team members' eyes, understanding both its negatives and positives, and to reframe and manage it productively.

Source of Difficulty	Related Sins	Your Role	Tips for Overcoming the Sin
Stakeholders assume we can add to the project scope at any time.	Creep, charity, excess, hope	Too lenient with stakeholder requests; reluctant to assert control and make tough decisions	Manage expectations, keeping stakeholders and sponsors informed as changes occur, noting their impact. Establish and follow a change control process.
Stakeholders are unrealistically optimistic in early stages and at project decision points.	Magical thinking, promises, ego, lateness, shoddy quality	Plans are made without realistic steps for execution; lessons learned are ignored	Be proactive about communicating project progress and challenges. Rely on objective measures to determine if commitments are being met at various stages of the project.

Adapted from *The Five Commitments of a Leader* by Mark Leheney. © 2008 by Management Concepts, Inc. All rights reserved.

About the Contributors

B. Michael Aucoin is the President of Leading Edge Management, LLC, and Electrical Expert, Inc., located in College Station, Texas. He is the author of *Right-Brain Project Management: A Complementary Approach* and *From Engineer to Manager: Mastering the Transition*.

Sanjiv Augustine is the President of LitheSpeed, an agile and lean training, consulting, and coaching firm. He is an industry-leading agile and lean expert, cofounder of the Agile Project Leadership Network (APLN), and author of *Managing Agile Projects*. He is also the founder and moderator of the Yahoo! agile project management discussion group.

Richard Bechtold, PhD, is an independent software project management consultant specializing in process improvement and implementing and appraising processes that are compliant with the CMMI (Capability Maturity Model Integration), ISO 9000-2008, AS 9100, and other quality standards and frameworks. Dr. Bechtold is an SEI (Software Engineering Institute, Carnegie Mellon University) Authorized Lead Appraiser.

Gayle L. Brennan, PMP, has managed project teams and participated on major projects throughout an extensive telecommunications industry career. She is currently involved in contract administration and managing major contract compliance projects.

Charlene Spoede Budd, PhD, PMP, is a Professor Emeritus at Baylor University and owner of Budd Management Systems. She is the coauthor of *A Practical Guide to Earned Value Project Management.*

Charles I. Budd, PMP, is a principal with Budd Management Systems in Atlanta, Georgia. He is also a Director for Angel Systems, Inc., the provider of an electronic medical records system for the behavioral healthcare industry. He is currently developing project management automation tools, consulting on information systems projects, and conducting seminars. He is the coauthor of *A Practical Guide to Earned Value Project Management.*

Janet Burns, PMP, is an independent project management consultant and trainer, specializing in project management process and methodology implementation. She has extensive experience managing large software projects and enterprise-wide process improvement projects. She is a past president of the Hampton Roads chapter of the Project Management Institute and was recently named to the PMI® Power 50.

Michael S. Dobson, PMP, has over 25 years of operating project management experience in a variety of fields. He helped build the Smithsonian's National Air and Space Museum and directed marketing and game development for a leading hobby company. He is a well-known author of project management books, including *The Six Dimensions of Project Management.*

Lowell D. Dye, PMP, is a senior consultant and trainer with experience in manufacturing, insurance, research and development, defense, and several other industries. He has published and spoken widely on various project management topics.

Steven Flannes, PhD, is the principal of Flannes & Associates (www.flannesandassociates.com). He is the coauthor of *Essen-*

tial People Skills for Project Managers and presents seminars on people skills in project management throughout the United States, Canada, and Europe.

Ken Hanley, MEng (Project Management), is the principal of KTH Program and Project Management Inc., a Calgary-based consulting firm specializing in project management and information technologies. He teaches graduate courses on project management in the Faculties of Engineering and Management at the University of Calgary and writes and speaks frequently on information technology, management, and project management.

Kathleen B. (Kitty) Hass, PMP, is a senior practice consultant specializing in the project management and business analysis disciplines. She is a prominent presenter at industry conferences and the author of *Managing Complex Projects: A New Model* and the *Business Analysis Essential Library* series.

Dr. Gregory T. Haugan, PMP, has over 40 years of experience as a project manager in both the private and public sectors. He is a Vice President of GLH, Inc., providing consulting services specializing in proposal preparation and project start-up. He is the author of *Project Management Fundamentals: Key Concepts and Methodology* and *Work Breakdown Structures for Projects, Programs, and Enterprises.*

Gary R. Heerkens, PMP, CPM, CBM, CIPA, PE, MBA, is president of Management Solutions Group, a project management training and consulting firm he started after managing projects at Eastman Kodak for over 20 years. He is a columnist for *PM Network* magazine, was a four-term president of the Rochester Chapter of PMI, and is the author of *The Business-Savvy Project Manager* and *Project Management: 24 Lessons to Help You Master Any Project.*

Dr. David Hillson, PMP, HonFAPM, FIRM, FRSA, FCMI, known worldwide as "The Risk Doctor," works internationally as a consultant, trainer, speaker, and author specializing in risk management. He is best known for promoting inclusion of opportunity in the risk process, and he has also developed a unique approach to understanding and managing risk attitudes.

Rosemary Hossenlopp, PMP, is a Silicon Valley–based consultant who focuses on assessing and improving IT project practices. She has 20 years of experience directing complex commercial and government projects and initiatives.

Brian Irwin, MSM, PMP, works with large organizations on the creation and deployment of project portfolio management initiatives. He has over 15 years of project and program management experience and is an active PMI volunteer and speaker. He is the author of *Managing Politics and Conflict in Projects*.

John K. Johnson, MBA, CPA, has over 35 years of experience as a project manager in both the private and public sectors. He provides business consulting services, specializing in finance and accounting.

John Kinser, PMP, has over 35 years of experience as a project manager, engineer, consultant, and trainer. His work in the construction, manufacturing, IT, and training industries worldwide has given him a keen understanding of the variety of skills needed, and challenges faced, by today's project managers.

Timothy J. Kloppenborg, PhD, PMP, is a Castellini Distinguished Professor at Xavier University in Cincinnati. He is a retired Air Force Reserve officer who has worked on construction, quality improvement, IT, and R&D projects. He is the author of *Contemporary Project Management, Project Leadership,* and *Managing Project Quality.*

Ursula Kuehn, PMP, EVP, is president of UQN and Associates, a consulting and training firm, and the author of *Integrated Cost and Schedule Control in Project Management.*

Dr. Ginger Levin, PMP, PgMP, Certified *OPM3* Assessor, is a consultant and educator in program and project management. Her areas of specialization are portfolio management, the project management office, metrics, and maturity assessments.

Michael F. Malinowski, PMP, has more than 24 years of IT project management and programming experience. He is the author of *IT Maintenance: Applied Project Management.*

Michael G. Martin, PMP, is an internationally recognized consultant, speaker, trainer, and author with extensive experience in enterprise risk management and portfolio, program, and project management. He is the past president of the Atlanta PMI chapter, member of the PMP® exam development committee, founding chair of the PMI® government specific-interest group, and author of *Delivering Project Excellence with the Statement of Work* and *Federal Statements of Work: A Practical Guide.*

Dr. Jerry Mulenburg, PMP, was a project manager for NASA and the U.S. Air Force and has worked in a number of senior management positions related to project management. His education includes a doctorate in business administration, an MS in both systems management and aerospace engineering, and a BS in aero-mechanical engineering.

Steve Neuendorf is an independent consultant, author, and speaker in the areas of IT project management and measurement. He is the author of *Project Measurement* and *Six Sigma for Project Managers.*

Michael O'Brochta, PMP, led efforts to create mature project management practices throughout the Central Intelligence

Agency. As president of Zozer, Inc., he is helping organizations raise their level of project management performance.

Frank R. Parth, MS, MSSM, MBA, PMP, president of Project Auditors, LLC, has 30 years of experience in various aspects of project management. He served as PMI's project manager for the *Standard for Program Management, Second Edition*, and is the coauthor of *Introduction to IT Project Management*.

Joseph A. Petrick is the Brage Golding Distinguished Professor of Management Research in the Department of Management and International Business and Executive Director of the Institute for Business Integrity at the Raj Soin College of Business at Wright State University. He is also CEO of Performance Leadership Associates, an international consulting and training firm specializing in quality and project management services, and Integrity Capacity Associates, an international consulting and training firm specializing in diagnosing and developing the ethical work cultures of organizations. He is the coauthor of *Managing Project Quality*.

Sandra F. Rowe, PMP, MBA, MSCIS, has over 20 years of project management experience. Her responsibilities have included leading IT and process improvement projects; developing project management processes, tools, and techniques; and designing, developing, and delivering project management training programs. She speaks regularly on project management processes, project management for small projects, and the project office and is the author of *Project Management for Small Projects*.

Amy R. Scarbrough is director of a newly created department to support the expansion of internal company activities in the areas of business analysis, process improvement, and knowledge management. She is highly experienced in program evaluation, qualitative and quantitative analysis, and public policy research.

Peter Simon, PMP, FAPM, is a Managing Partner with the UK firm Lucidus Consulting. He has over 30 years of project management experience across most industries and business sectors. He is a Visiting Fellow of the Cranfield School of Management.

Ray Stratton, PMP, EVP, is founder and president of Management Technologies (www.mgmt-technologies.com), a program management training and consulting firm. He does consulting and training in earned value management (EVM), with a focus on IT systems, ANSI 748 compliance, and simplified EVM implementations. He is the author of *The Earned Value Management Maturity Model*®.

Jerry Strauss, PMP, PE, has managed environmental and engineering projects for over 35 years, ranging in size up to $34 million. He has organized and developed project management offices for two engineering companies.

Ron Taylor, MBA, PMP, is principal of the Ron Taylor Group and was president of the PMI Washington, D.C., chapter (PMI-WDC) in 2007–2008. PMIWDC is the largest PMI chapter in the world, with over 8,500 members. During Mr. Taylor's term as president, PMIWDC was named PMI Chapter of the Year and he was named PMI Leader of the Year.

Michael Trumper has worked in the fields of technical communications, marketing, and software development for the past 18 years. Over the past 10 years he has been involved in projects involving economic valuation and risk and project lifecycle modeling. He is the coauthor of *Project Decisions: The Art and Science.*

Teidi Tucker, director of west coast business development, has more than 21 years of experience in many facets of business, including project management, business analysis, technical training, information technology, and financial services.

Nathalie Udo, MBA, PMP, founder of Projectway, LLC, has a proven record of accomplishments in leading complex international software development and implementation projects for corporations like Baan Company, Boeing Corporation, and Kaiser Permanente. She is a seasoned professional with extensive project management, cross-cultural communication, and leadership skills.

Lev Virine has more than 20 years of experience as a structural engineer, software developer, and project manager. In the past 10 years he has been involved in a number of major projects performed by Fortune 500 companies and government agencies to establish effective decision analysis and risk management processes as well as to conduct risk analyses of complex projects. He is the coauthor of *Project Decisions: The Art and Science.*

Ralph Young is a constant, positive advocate of best practices who encourages individuals, projects, and organizations to commit to and practice continuous improvement. Visit his website, www.ralphyoung.net.

Related Project Management Resources

Aucoin, B. Michael, *From Engineer to Manager: Mastering the Transition* (Boston: Artech House, 2002).

Aucoin, B. Michael, *Right-Brain Project Management: A Complementary Approach* (Vienna, VA: Management Concepts, 2007).

Augustine, Sanjiv, *Managing Agile Projects* (Upper Saddle River, NJ: Prentice Hall PTR, 2005).

Bechtold, Richard, *Essentials of Software Project Management, Second Edition* (Vienna, VA: Management Concepts, 2007).

Budd, Charles, and Charlene Budd, *A Practical Guide to Earned Value Management, Second Edition* (Vienna, VA: Management Concepts, 2009).

Budd, Charlene, and Charles Budd, *Reporting and Improvement Initiatives* (Washington, D.C.: Bureau of National Affairs, 2007).

Dobson, Michael S., *Practical Project Management: The Secrets of Managing Any Project on Time and on Budget* (Mission, KS: SkillPath Publications, 1996).

Dobson, Michael S., *Project Management for the Technical Professional* (Newtown Square, PA: Project Management Institute, 2001).

Dobson, Michael S., *The Six Dimensions of Project Management: Turning Constraints into Resources* (Vienna, VA: Management Concepts, 2007).

Dobson, Michael S., *The Triple Constraints in Project Management*, a volume in *The Project Management Essential Library* (Vienna, VA: Management Concepts, 2004).

Dye, Lowell, and James Pennypacker, eds., *Project Portfolio Management: Selecting and Prioritizing Projects for Competitive Advantage* (West Chester, PA: Center for Business Practices, 2003).

Hass, Kathleen B., *Business Analysis Essential Library* series (Vienna, VA: Management Concepts, 2007).

Hass, Kathleen B., *Managing Complex Projects: A New Model* (Vienna, VA: Management Concepts, 2008).

Haugan, Gregory T., *Project Management Fundamentals: Key Concepts and Methodology* (Vienna, VA: Management Concepts, 2006).

Haugan, Gregory T., *Work Breakdown Structures for Projects, Programs, and Enterprises* (Vienna, VA: Management Concepts, 2008).

Heerkens, Gary, *The Business-Savvy Project Manager* (McGraw-Hill Professional, 2007).

Heerkens, Gary, *Project Management (The Briefcase Book series)* (McGraw-Hill Professional, 2001).

Heerkens, Gary, *Project Management: 24 Lessons to Help You Master Any Project* (McGraw-Hill Professional, 2004).

Hillson, David, *Effective Opportunity Management for Projects: Exploiting Positive Risk* (Boca Raton, FL: Taylor & Francis, 2004).

Hillson, David, *Managing Risk in Projects*, in *Fundamentals in Project Management* series, ed. D. Dalcher (Farnham, UK: Gower, 2009).

Hillson David (ed.). *The Risk Management Universe: A Guided Tour* (London: British Standards Institution, 2007).

Hillson, David, and Ruth Murray-Webster, *Understanding and Managing Risk Attitude, Second Edition* (Farnham, UK: Gower, 2007).

Hillson, David, and Peter Simon, *Practical Project Risk Management: The ATOM Methodology* (Vienna, VA: Management Concepts, 2007).

Hossenlopp, Rosemary, *Unearthing Business Requirements: Elicitation Tools and Techniques*, a volume in the *Business Analysis Essential Library* (Vienna, VA: Management Concepts, 2008).

Irwin, Brian, *Managing Politics and Conflict in Projects* (Vienna, VA: Management Concepts, 2008).

Kloppenborg, Timothy, *Contemporary Project Management* (Stamford, CT: South-Western College Publishing/Cengage, 2008).

Kloppenborg, Timothy, Arthur Shriberg, and Jayashree Venkatraman, *Project Leadership*, a volume in the *Project Management Essential Library* (Vienna, VA: Management Concepts, 2003).

Kloppenborg, Timothy, and Joseph Petrick, *Managing Project Quality*, a volume in the *Project Management Essential Library* (Vienna, VA: Management Concepts, 2002).

Kuehn, Ursula, *Integrated Cost and Schedule Control in Project Management* (Vienna, VA: Management Concepts, 2006).

Levin, Ginger, and Steven W. Flannes, *Essential People Skills for Project Managers* (Vienna, VA: Management Concepts, 2005).

Levin, Ginger, and Allen Green, *Implementing Program Management: Templates for Success* (Boca Raton, FL: Taylor & Francis, CRC Press, 2009).

Malinowski, Michael, *IT Maintenance: Applied Project Management* (Vienna, VA: Management Concepts, 2007).

Martin, Michael, *Delivering Project Excellence with the Statement of Work* (Vienna, VA: Management Concepts, 2003).

Martin, Michael, *Federal Statements of Work* (Vienna, VA: Management Concepts, 2008).

Murray-Webster, Ruth, and David Hillson, *Managing Group Risk Attitude* (Farnham, UK: Gower, 2008).

Neuendorf, Steve, *Project Measurement*, a volume in the *Project Management Essential Library* (Vienna, VA: Management Concepts, 2002).

Neuendorf, Steve, *Six Sigma for Project Managers*, a volume in the *Project Management Essential Library* (Vienna, VA: Management Concepts, 2004).

Pennypacker, James, and Lowell Dye, *Managing Multiple Projects: Planning, Scheduling, and Allocating Resources for Competitive Advantage* (New York: Marcel Dekker, 2002).

Petrick, Joseph, and John F. Quinn, *Managing Ethics: Integrity at Work*, SAGE series on Business Ethics (Thousand Oaks, CA: Sage Publications, 1997).

Rad, Parviz F., and Ginger Levin, *Achieving Project Management Success Using Virtual Teams* (Ft. Lauderdale, FL: J. Ross Publishing, 2003).

Rad, Parviz F., and Ginger Levin, *The Advanced Project Management Office: A Comprehensive Look at Function and Implementation* (Boca Raton, FL: CRC Press, 2002).

Rad, Parviz F., and Ginger Levin, *Metrics for Project Managers* (Vienna, VA: Management Concepts, 2005).

Rad, Parviz F., and Ginger Levin, *Project Portfolio Management: Tools and Techniques* (New York: IIL Publishing, 2007).

Rowe, Sandra, *Project Management for Small Projects* (Vienna, VA: Management Concepts, 2007).

Snyder, Cynthia, and Frank Parth, *Introduction to IT Project Management* (Vienna, VA: Management Concepts, 2007).

Snyder, Cynthia, and Frank Parth, *Introduction to IT Project Management Forms* (Vienna, VA: Management Concepts, 2007).

Solomon, Paul J., and Ralph R. Young, *Performance-Based Earned Value* (Hoboken, NJ: John Wiley & Sons, Copyright IEEE Computer Society, 2007).

Stratton, Ray W., *The Earned Value Management Maturity Model®* (Vienna, VA: Management Concepts, 2006).

Virine, Lev, and Michael Trumper, *Project Decisions: The Art and Science* (Vienna, VA: Management Concepts, 2008).

Ward, LeRoy, and Ginger Levin, *PgMP Study Guide* (Arlington,VA: ESI, 2008).

Ward, LeRoy, and Ginger Levin, *PMP Challenge* (Arlington,VA: ESI, 2004).

Young, Ralph, *Effective Requirements Practices* (Boston: Addison-Wesley, 2001).

Young, Ralph, *Project Requirements: A Guide to Best Practices* (Vienna, VA: Management Concepts, 2006).

Young, Ralph, *The Requirements Engineering Handbook* (Boston: Artech House, 2004).

Young, Ralph R., Steven Brady, and Dennis Nagle, *How to Save a Failing Project: Chaos to Control* (Vienna, VA: Management Concepts, 2009).

CPSIA information can be obtained at www.ICGtesting.com
Printed in the USA
BVOW082133181212

308592BV00004B/8/P